SOMETIMES YOU WIN— SOMETIMES YOU LEARN

Books by Dr. John C. Maxwell
Can Teach You How to Be a REAL Success

Relationships

25 Ways to Win with People

Becoming a Person of Influence

Encouragement Changes Everything

Ethics 101

Everyone Communicates, Few Connect

The Power of Partnership

Relationships 101

Winning with People

Attitude

Attitude 101

The Difference Maker

Failing Forward

How Successful People Think

Success 101

Thinking for a Change

The Winning Attitude

Equipping

The 17 Essential Qualities of a Team Player

The 17 Indisputable Laws of Teamwork

Developing the Leaders around You

Equipping 101

Make Today Count

Mentoring 101

My Dream Map

Partners in Prayer

Put Your Dream to the Test

Running with the Giants

Talent Is Never Enough

Today Matters

Your Road Map for Success

Leadership

The 5 Levels of Leadership

The 15 Invaluable Laws of Growth

The 10th Anniversary Edition of The 21 Irrefutable Laws of Leadership

The 21 Indispensable Qualities of a Leader

The 21 Most Powerful Minutes in a Leader's Day

The 360 Degree Leader

Developing the Leader within You

Go for Gold

How Successful People Lead

Leadership 101

Leadership Gold

Leadership Promises for Every Day

— SOMETIMES YOU —
WIN
— SOMETIMES YOU —
LEARN

LIFE'S GREATEST LESSONS ARE
GAINED FROM OUR LOSSES

JOHN C. MAXWELL

**CENTER
STREET**

NEW YORK   BOSTON   NASHVILLE

The author is represented by Yates & Yates, LLP,
Literary Agency, Orange, California.

Center Street
Hachette Book Group USA
237 Park Avenue
New York, NY 10017

Visit our website at www.centerstreet.com

The Center Street name and logo are registered trademarks of the Hachette Book Group USA.
Printed in the United States of America

First edition: October 2013
10   9   8   7   6   5   4   3   2   1

Library of Congress Cataloging-in-Publication Data

Maxwell, John C.
   Sometimes you win—sometimes you learn : life's greatest lessons are gained from our losses / John C. Maxwell. — First edition.
      pages cm
   Includes bibliographical references.
   ISBN 978-1-59995-369-4 (hardback) — ISBN 978-1-4555-7611-1 (large print hardcover) — ISBN 978-1-60788-519-1 (audiobook)   1. Failure (Psychology)   2. Experience.   I. Title.

   BF575.F14M39 2013
   158—dc23

                                                      2013022012

*To Paul Martinelli, Scott Fay, and
the thousands of coaches around the world
who are part of The John Maxwell Team:*

You share my heart.

You communicate my values.

You live out my vision.

*You are adding value to others far beyond
my hopes and expectations.*

*Thank you for creating a legacy for me
while I'm still around to see it.*

Contents

A Note from the Author

For many years, I had the opportunity of meeting regularly with former UCLA basketball coach John Wooden. I'd spend a day preparing to meet with him, deciding what questions I would ask. I was very conscious of how rare a privilege it was to learn from a mentor such as him.

Coach was always so kind and thoughtful. The last time I met with him, he asked me what I was working on. I had just finished the outline for *Sometimes You Win—Sometimes You Learn*, and I was very excited about it. I took the pages from my briefcase and showed them to him, detailing the thesis and what had prompted me to write it.

"What a tremendous idea. You can help people with this," said Coach. Then he really surprised me. He asked, "Can I write the foreword for it?"

What an honor! Of course I said yes.

Coach wrote the foreword as promised, and a few months later he died. I was very humbled, realizing that this was one of the last things he probably wrote.

The world of book writing is a funny thing. My publisher decided that they wanted me to write *The 5 Levels of Leadership* first, then

The 15 Invaluable Laws of Growth. During that time, this book had to wait. After a delay of a couple of years, I finally got to write it.

So that's the story of how John Wooden came to write the following foreword. I am grateful for his thoughts. He may have gone on before us, but he is surely not forgotten.

Foreword by Coach John Wooden

John C. Maxwell is a man I am proud to call my friend.

It isn't just that he has authored more than fifty books on leadership and character, though that is pretty impressive. It isn't just that his words of encouragement have inspired millions of people to reevaluate their choices and priorities, though that is important. It isn't just that he is a man of principles and faith, though those are admirable qualities. I am proud to call John my friend because he is a man who understands that above all things, life is about learning—and about using those lessons to become a better employer, better employee, better parent, better sibling, better friend, better neighbor, better steward of our blessings.

This philosophy has been the bedrock of my own life, and I credit John with always serving as a wonderful reminder of how much more learning can be done. I never saw myself as a coach but rather as a teacher whose primary classroom was the basketball court. But I also understood that I was an eternal student, as well. I have tried every day to learn something new, to gain a different perspective, or to harbor a more mature understanding of the world. That way of thinking is what keeps a mind young, optimistic, and joyful. Every time John would visit me, his yellow legal pad covered with the questions he planned to ask me, I always got a chuckle at the sight of one of the professional world's leading answer men still eager for deeper insights and still willing to ask questions to gain them. It was a wonderful reminder that I should do the same.

After all, learning isn't something that stops when we are handed a diploma. In fact, that's actually the point when the real learning begins. The lessons we are given in school are not the things that carry us through life; those are just the lessons that give us the basic tools to face the real world outside the classroom walls. And that real world is going to sting. It is going to hurt. Sometimes it is going to bump and bruise you; other times it is going to knock you off your feet. The losses are going to come at you in every shape and size, and hit you in every area of your life from your finances to your heart to your health, and more—that much is guaranteed. What is not guaranteed is how you react to those challenges.

As John discusses in this book, there is a marked difference between the people who learn from their losses and the people who do not. Do you want your spirit stuck in the infirmary, too battle weary for another try? Or do you want to seize the opportunity to study, evaluate, and reconsider what happened—and use that knowledge to arm yourself for another charge at life?

The elements of learning that John outlines in the following pages are profound observations as to how the process happens, and he pinpoints what character trait or attribute comes from each. By dissecting the "DNA of those who learn," as he so succinctly puts it, John walks us through the necessary components of dealing with different types of loss and turning those lessons into valuable weapons both to ward off and fight through future challenges.

I would challenge anyone who has ever suffered a setback, felt disappointment, or been the recipient of bad news (in other words, every human who has ever walked the earth) to read John's message and not find at least one insight that can drastically change his or her own perspective on life's darker moments.

If we follow John's advice and learn to look at losses as opportunities for growth through learning, then we become undefeatable. Life will always be fraught with loss, but if we are properly armed, the loss will not overcome us. Because the man or woman who takes something worthwhile from the bad times strips them of their control over our minds, bodies, hearts, and souls.

These pages offer more than just a how-to manual for getting through difficult times; they offer the most valuable gift of all: hope.

Acknowledgments

Thank you to:
Charlie Wetzel, my writer;
Stephanie Wetzel, my social media manager;
Linda Eggers, my executive assistant.

SOMETIMES YOU WIN—
SOMETIMES YOU LEARN

1

When You're Losing, Everything Hurts

My friend Robert Schuller once asked, "What would you attempt to do if you knew you wouldn't fail?" That's a great question, an inspiring question. When most people hear it, they start dreaming again. They are motivated to reach for their goals and to risk more.

I have a question that I think is just as important: what do you learn when you fail?

While people are usually ready to talk about their dreams, they are not well prepared to answer a question about their shortcomings. Most people don't like to talk about their mistakes and failures. They don't want to confront their losses. They are embarrassed by them. And when they do find themselves falling short, they may find themselves saying something trite, such as "Sometimes you win, sometimes you lose." The message is, "Hope to win, expect to lose, and live with the results either way."

What's wrong with that? It's not how winners think!

Successful people approach losing differently. They don't try to brush failure under the rug. They don't run away from their losses.

Their attitude is never *Sometimes you win, sometimes you lose.* Instead they think, *Sometimes you win, sometimes you learn.* They understand that life's greatest lessons are gained from our losses—if we approach them the right way.

This One Really Hurt

I've experienced many wins in life, but I've also had more than my share of losses. Some losses came through no fault of my own. However, many were of my own making, coming from bad choices and dumb mistakes. On March 12, 2009, I made the mother of all stupid mistakes. I tried to go through security at a major airport with a forgotten handgun in my briefcase. That is a federal offense! It was by far the dumbest thing I've ever done. Here's how it came about.

The previous Saturday, I was in Birmingham, Alabama, speaking at the Church of the Highlands. It's a wonderful church with a marvelous leader named Chris Hodges. He is a good friend who serves on the board of EQUIP, the not-for-profit organization I founded to teach leadership internationally. Chris's people are fantastic, and I had a terrific time with them that weekend.

Many times when I have a speaking engagement, I fly commercially. But whenever the engagement isn't far away from home and it means that I would be able to come home and sleep in my own bed, I try to fly on a private airplane. That was the case following my time with Chris in Birmingham.

As I was about to get on the plane at the general aviation airport to fly home, a friend of Chris's who had ridden with us wanted to give me a gift: a Beretta pistol.

"This is for Margaret," he said, "so she can feel safe when you're traveling."

I have friends who know a lot about guns. Some do a lot of hunting. And I've gone hunting with friends several times. I've shot rifles and shotguns, but I don't really know a lot about guns. And to be honest, they don't have great interest to me. I'm not really pro- or antigun. I just don't think a lot about them. And I'm not a technical person. But I knew this pistol had been given as a gift from the heart, so I accepted it and put it in my briefcase.

After we landed, the pilot remarked on what a nice gun it was. And he asked me, "Do you know how to load it?"

"I have no idea," I answered.

"Let me do it for you," he said.

He loaded the gun, made sure it was secure, and gave it back to me. I put it back in my briefcase and went home.

And then I forgot all about it.

The next several days were very busy for me. I had a commitment to speak to a large group in Dallas, and I was entirely focused on getting ready for it. There was one brief moment while I was working on my lesson when I thought to myself, *Oh, I need to remember to get that gun out of my bag.* But I was in the middle of writing, and I didn't want to stop because I was on a roll. So I thought, *I'll do it later.*

Time passed. Life was busy. I kept working. And before I knew it, Thursday morning rolled around and off I went to the airport.

If you're my age, you may remember a cartoon character named Mr. Magoo. He was a man who seemed to wander from danger to danger without ever getting hurt. Some of my friends used to call me Mr. Magoo. (If you're not old enough to know Mr. Magoo, maybe you remember Forrest Gump. Friends have called me that, too.)

On that Thursday, in my worst Mr. Magoo moment, I strolled right up to security and dropped my briefcase on the conveyer belt. Just as I was about to walk through the metal detector, I remembered the gun.

In a panic I blurted out, "There's a gun in there! There's a gun in there!"

Truly, it is one of the stupidest things I have ever done. I felt like an idiot. And to make matters worse, many of the people who were at the security checkpoint knew me, including the man who operated the screening device. He said, "Mr. Maxwell, I am sorry but I will have to report this." Trust me, that came as no surprise. They stopped everything, shut down the conveyor belt, handcuffed me, and took me away.

It turned out that the head of the sheriff's division who filled out the police report knew me too. He was all business for about an hour. But then after we had completed the procedure, he turned to me, smiled, and said, "I love your books. If I had known we would meet up like this, I would have brought them here for you to sign."

"If you could get me out of this mess, I'd give you signed books for the rest of your life," I replied.

The man who took my mug shot knew me. When they brought me into the room where he worked, he said, "Mr. Maxwell, what are you doing here?"

He took the handcuffs off of me and told the officer that I didn't need them.

Needless to say, when he took my picture, I didn't smile.

Assessing the Loss

Immediately after being released on bail, I met my attorney, who said, "Our main goal is to keep this quiet."

"That's impossible," I responded, telling him of all the people I encountered who knew me during the entire ordeal. Sure enough, the news broke that evening. In order to let people know what happened and to minimize publicity damage, before the news broke I tweeted the following message: *Definition of Stupid: Receive a gun as a gift; Forget it's in carry-on and go to the airport. Security not happy!*

Too often in my life I have not been careful enough. I knew better than to put a gun in my briefcase. Immediately after security found the gun, I began silently lecturing myself about my

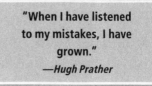

"When I have listened to my mistakes, I have grown."
—*Hugh Prather*

carelessness. The words of Hugh Prather fit me perfectly: "I sometimes react to making a mistake as if I have betrayed myself. My fear of making a mistake seems to be based on the hidden assumption that I am potentially perfect, and that if I can just be very careful I will not fall from heaven. But a mistake is a declaration of the way I am, a jolt to the way I intend, a reminder that I am not dealing with facts. When I have listened to my mistakes, I have grown."

The words *be careful* have been my takeaway from this experience. Mistakes are acceptable as long as the damage isn't too great. Or as they say in Texas, "It doesn't matter how much milk you spill as long as you don't lose your cow!"

I am convinced that we are all one step away from stupid. I could have "lost my cow" because of this incident. None of us does life so well that we are far away from doing something dumb. And what it has taken a lifetime to build has the potential to be lost in a moment. My hope was that a lifetime of striving to live with integrity would outweigh an act of stupidity.

Fortunately, as soon as the story became public, my friends started to rally around me and support me. Because I knew that people would begin asking questions about it, I immediately wrote about it on my blog, JohnMaxwellonLeadership.com, in a post called "Stupid Is as

Stupid Does." The supportive response from people was overwhelming. Their words of encouragement and prayers certainly lifted my spirit.

Other friends took a more humorous approach to me. When I went to speak at the Crystal Cathedral, Gretchen Schuller said, "John, security wants to pat you down before you speak." Bill Hybels wrote me a note that said, "No sex? No money scandal? Boring..." Angela Williams e-mailed my assistant, Linda Eggers, with these words: "Tell John he's my hero. His estimation has risen in my eyes. I come from a long line of 'Bubbas.' Lots of pistol-packing men and women. Art's mom was arrested in the Atlanta airport in the '80s for having a Clint Eastwood–type pistol in her large purse...she too forgot about it." And Jessamyn West pointed out, "It is very easy to forgive others their mistakes; it takes more grit and gumption to forgive them for having witnessed your own."

Then I started to receive people's suggestions for the title of my next book, including:

- Developing the Gangsta within You
- 21 Irrefutable Laws of Airport Security
- The 21 Indisputable, Irrefutable Reasons Why Not to Forget Your Gun in Your Briefcase When Going to the Airport
- Leading from the Middle of the Gang
- Have Gun, Will Travel

Today, I feel very fortunate because the incident was dismissed by the court and it has been expunged from my record. I can laugh about the whole thing. In fact, not long after the ordeal, I created a reminder for myself of the fact that in life sometimes you win, sometimes you learn. I often carry it in my briefcase (instead of a gun). It's a laminated card. On one side is the April 2009 cover of *Success Magazine*. I was featured on that cover, and I look great! Million-dollar smile. Blue suit. A posture of success and confidence. Half a million people bought that magazine, saw my picture, and read my words about success.

On the other side is my mug shot. It was taken only two weeks after the magazine came out! No million-dollar smile. No blue suit, just sweats. Poor posture and a look of complete discouragement. It just goes to show you that there's not much distance between the penthouse and the outhouse.

Why Losses Hurt So Much

In life, sometimes you win. In my younger years I played basketball and was very competitive. I liked to win, and I hated losing. When I was in my early twenties, I went to a class reunion, where I played in a game against other former players. We were all eager to prove we could still play at the same level, and it turned out to be a very physical game. Of course, I wanted to win, so I was very aggressive. After I knocked one opponent to the floor, he shouted in frustration, "Back off, it's only a game!"

My reply: "Then let me win."

I'm not exactly proud of that, but I think it illustrates how much most of us like to win. When we win, nothing hurts; when we lose, everything hurts. And the only time you hear someone use the phrase "It's only a game" is when that person is losing.

Think of some of the losses in your life and how they made you feel. Not good. And it's not just the pain of the moment that affects us. Our losses also cause us other difficulties. Here are a few:

1. Losses Cause Us to Be Emotionally Stuck

Author and speaker Les Brown says, "The good times we put in our pocket. The bad times we put in our heart." I have found that to be true in my life. In my heart I still carry some of the bad times. I bet you do too. The negative experiences affect us more deeply than positive ones, and if you're like me, you may get emotionally stuck.

> "The good times we put in our pocket. The bad times we put in our heart."
> —Les Brown

Recently I experienced being emotionally stuck after I made a foolish mistake. Ron Puryear, a wonderful friend, invited me to stay a few days at his beautiful river house in Idaho so that I could get away and begin writing this book. The setting is inspiring and perfect for thinking and writing. The view overlooks a beautiful body of water with tree-covered hills in the background. It's spectacular. Since I had speaking gigs in Spokane, Edmonton, and Los Angeles, all western cities, I decided to take him up on his offer.

My son-in-law Steve and our friend Mark were with me because they would be going with me to Edmonton, Canada. As we got into the car in Spokane, Washington, to head for the airport, Steve asked, "Do we all have our passports?" My heart sank! I had forgotten mine!

Now, this was no simple matter of turning around and going back to get it. I was out west and my passport was in Florida, more than two thousand miles away. In six hours, I was supposed to be speaking in Edmonton. I started to feel sick. What was I going to do?

How could an experienced, international traveler like me make such a foolish error? I felt like an idiot.

Steve, Mark, my assistant Linda, and I tried to solve my problem over the next two hours. Each passing minute revealed that I had a big problem. I knew I would not be allowed to board a plane to Canada without my passport. (Trust me. I asked!) We also discovered that we could not get the passport in time via air express. Nor would a family member in Florida be able to get on a commercial flight and bring it to me in time. I would not be able to fulfill my speaking commitment that night. The situation felt impossible to solve.

Finally after a lot of work and creative thinking we found a solution. Our host in Edmonton agreed to move my evening speaking engagement from that night to the following evening. Meanwhile, we hired a private jet to fly from Florida to Spokane with my passport. In my mind was a ridiculous picture of someone placing the passport in one of the seats, as if it were a passenger. Boy, did I feel stupid.

At midnight when the plane arrived, we got on board and continued on to Edmonton. We arrived the next morning, and I was there for the next day's meeting and the evening speaking engagement. We had made it.

The good news was that we had solved the problem. The bad news was that the price of fixing my mistake was $20,000!

The rest of that day, I was emotionally stuck. I continually asked myself:

How could a veteran traveler like me make such a rookie mistake?

How much inconvenience did I cause the people who had to move the meeting from one night to the next?

Why didn't I think about the passport twenty-four hours earlier so it would have cost me hundreds of dollars, instead of thousands?

What would I have done if we had not found a solution?

All these thoughts and questions exhausted me emotionally. To try to bounce back, I drank a milk shake (comfort food), went swimming, and tried to rest. But no matter what I did, I still continually kicked myself for being so dumb. I felt like a slave to my own moods and feelings.

I usually process through mistakes and failures pretty quickly, but I didn't feel free to do that this time. I was having a very tough time breaking out of my self-imposed prison of what-ifs. I can laugh about it today, but even now I still feel foolish for forgetting something so basic.

It's been said that if an ocean liner could think and feel, it would never leave its dock. It would be afraid of the thousands of huge waves it would have to encounter during its travels. Anxiety and fear are debilitating emotions for the human heart. So are losses. They can weaken, imprison, paralyze, dishearten, and sicken us. To be successful, we need to find ways to get unstuck emotionally.

2. Losses Cause Us to Be Mentally Defeated

Life is a succession of losses, beginning with the loss of the warmth and comfort of the womb that nurtured us for the first nine months of our existence. In childhood we lose the luxury of total dependence on our mothers. We lose our favorite toys. We lose days dedicated to play and exploration. We lose the privilege of pursuing the irresponsible pleasures of youth. We separate from the protection of our families as we leave the nest and take on adult responsibilities. Over the course of our adult lives, we lose jobs and positions. Our self-esteem may take a beating. We lose money. We miss opportunities. Friends and family die. And I don't even want to talk about some of the physical losses we experience with advancing age! We lose all these things and more, until we finally face the final loss—that of life itself. It cannot be denied that our lives are filled with loss. Some losses are great; some are small. And the losses we face affect our mental health. Some people handle it well, while others don't.

The quality that distinguishes a successful person from an unsuccessful one who is otherwise like him is the capacity to manage disappointment and loss. This is a challenge because losses can often defeat us mentally. I know I've had to fight that battle.

> The quality that distinguishes a successful person from an unsuccessful one who is otherwise like him is the capacity to manage disappointment and loss.

When that happens, our thinking becomes like that of Harry Neale, the coach of the Vancouver Canucks in the 1980s. He said, "Last year we couldn't win on the road and this year we can't win at home. I don't know where else to play!"

Too often losing goes to our heads. It defeats us, and we have trouble coming up with solutions to our challenges. As the losses build up, they become more of a burden. We regret the losses of yesterday. We fear the losses of tomorrow. Regret saps our energy. We can't build on regret. Fear for the future distracts us and fills us with apprehension.

We want success, but we should instead train for losses. Author J. Wallace Hamilton echoed this when he wrote in *Leadership* magazine, "The increase of suicides, alcoholics, and even some forms of nervous breakdowns is evidence that many people are training for success when they should be training for failure. Failure is far more common than success; poverty is more prevalent than wealth; and disappointment more normal than arrival."

We need to expect mistakes, failures, and losses in life, since each of us will face many of them. But we need to take them as they come, not allow them to build up. As printer William A. Ward said, "Man, like a bridge, was designed to carry the load for a moment, not the combined weight of a year all at once."

3. Losses Create a Gap between I Should and I Did

Winning creates a positive cycle in our lives. When we win, we gain confidence. The more confidence we have, the more likely we are to take action when it's needed. That inclination to move from knowing to acting often brings success.

However, losing can also create a cycle in our lives—a negative one. Losses, especially when they pile up, can lead to insecurity. When we are insecure, we doubt ourselves. It causes us to hesitate when making decisions. Even if we know what we should do, we are reluctant to do it. When such a gap is created and isn't overcome, success becomes nearly impossible.

As I reflect on my losses and think about how they have affected me, I see that there have been times that they made me get stuck. I find that often occurs to others as well. Here are eleven traps that people tend to fall into:

- **The Mistake Trap:** "I'm afraid of doing something wrong." Losses hold us back!
- **The Fatigue Trap:** "I'm tired today." Losses wear us out.
- **The Comparison Trap:** "Someone else is better qualified than I am." Losses cause us to feel inferior to others.
- **The Timing Trap:** "This isn't the right time." Losses make us hesitate.
- **The Inspiration Trap:** "I don't feel like doing it right now." Losses demotivate us.
- **The Rationalization Trap:** "Maybe it's really not that important." Losses allow us to lose perspective.
- **The Perfection Trap:** "There's a best way to do it and I have to find it before I start." Losses cause us to question ourselves.

- **The Expectation Trap:** "I thought it would be easy, but it isn't." Losses highlight the difficulties.
- **The Fairness Trap:** "I shouldn't have to be the one to do this." Losses cause us to ask, "Why me?"
- **The Public Opinion Trap:** "If I fail, what will others think?" Losses paralyze us.
- **The Self-Image Trap:** "If I fail at this, it means I am a failure." Losses negatively affect how we see ourselves.

All of these traps are caused by losses, and all of them create the gap between knowing and doing. If we want to be successful, we need to bridge that gap.

4. The First Loss Often Isn't the Biggest Loss

When we experience a loss, we have a choice. If we immediately respond to it the right way, the loss becomes smaller to us. However if we respond the wrong way, or we fail to respond at all, that loss becomes greater. And it often leads to other losses. As the subsequent losses come at us, they seem to be bigger and bigger, crashing over us like waves in a violent storm. As the number of losses goes up, our self-confidence goes down.

We make matters worse when we compare ourselves to others, because we rarely do so on a level playing field. We either compare our best, including our good intentions, to someone else's worst, or we compare our worst to someone else's best. That can lead to a negative cycle of self-talk. But there's something you need to know:

The most important person you ever talk to is yourself, so be careful what you say.

The most important person that you will evaluate is yourself, so be
careful what you think.

The most important person you will love is yourself, so be careful
what you do.

> The most important
> person you ever talk to
> is yourself, so be careful
> what you say.

Yoga teacher and writer Kripalva-
nanda said, "My beloved child, break
your heart no longer. Each time you
judge yourself, you break your own
heart." I believe that in times of loss,
it's easy to get caught up in thinking about how we could have or
should have done things differently. Our self-talk can become very
negative. The more negative it becomes, the larger our losses appear
to be to us. If our self-talk is angry, destructive, or guilt producing, we
become even less capable of breaking free of the negative cycle.

If we can overcome an early loss and not let it become magnified,
that can help us move forward. That's not always easy to do, but even
someone who has faced a very great loss can learn to do it. I once read
that General Robert E. Lee visited the beautiful home of a wealthy
Kentucky widow after the Civil War. During their visit, she showed
him what was left of a magnificent old tree that hade been badly dam-
aged by Union artillery fire. The woman told Lee about the impact of
its loss to her, expecting him to sympathize. Instead, after a long pause
he advised, "Cut it down, my dear madam, and forget it."[1] He advised
her to move on. We also need to learn how to do that in a positive way.

5. Losses Never Leave Us the Same

Coaches of sports teams live in a world of wins and losses. Legendary football coach Knute Rockne quipped, "One loss is good for the

soul. Too many losses are not good for the coach." And longtime major league manager Paul Richards said, "If you can say the morale of your club is good after losing ten out of twelve games, then your intelligence is a little low."

> "If you can say the morale of your club is good after losing ten out of twelve games, then your intelligence is a little low."
> —*Paul Richards*

But you don't have to be a coach or play on a sports team to feel the impact of a loss.

I vividly remember a counseling session I had years ago with a man who was alienated from his brother. They hadn't talked to one another in years. As I listened to my client and watched him, I could feel the anger mounting in him as he recalled the details of their conflict. It finally came to a crescendo with these words, "Look what he's done to me. Look what he's done to me!"

In silence, I waited until he calmed down and was ready to listen. I calmly said, "Look what you're doing to yourself!"

Had he been wronged? Yes! But he was taking a bad experience and making the loss much worse.

The number or severity of your losses isn't as important as how you experience those losses. Yes, all losses hurt. And they make an impact on us, an impact that is rarely positive. Losses change us. But we must not allow them to control us. We can't let the fear of looking silly or incompetent paralyze us. We can't let the fear of negative consequences keep us from taking risks. Allowing negative experiences of the past to warp your future is like living in a coffin. It puts a lid on you and can end your life.

An ancient Greek legend tells of an athlete who ran well, but placed only second in his most important race. The crowd celebrated the winner and eventually erected a statue in his honor. Meanwhile, the man who had placed second came to think of himself as a loser. Envy ate away at him. He could think of nothing else but his defeat and his hatred for the winner who had bested him. Every day that he saw the statue, it reminded him of his lost opportunity for glory. So he decided to destroy it.

Late one night he went to the statue and chiseled at its base to weaken it. He returned in subsequent nights, working on it little by little. Still the statue remained standing. With each day, he became more annoyed. Then one night as he swung the hammer angrily, he went too far. The heavy marble statue finally broke loose. It crashed down upon him with all its weight, killing him instantly. He had turned his minor loss into a fatal one.

How does one minimize the negative damage of debilitating losses? First, by letting them go emotionally. In 1995 when Jerry Stackhouse was a rookie with the NBA's Philadelphia 76ers, he was asked about his take on life now that he was playing professional basketball. His answer: "Win and forget. Lose and forget." If we want to overcome adversity and keep from being defeated by our losses, we need to get past them. And then we need to learn from them!

Turning a Loss into a Gain

If you're going to lose—and you are because everyone does—then why not turn it into a gain? How do you do that? By learning from it. A loss isn't totally a loss if you learn something as a result of it. Your losses can come to define you if you let them. If you stay where a loss leaves you, then eventually you can get stuck there. But know this: your choices will begin to declare you. You can choose to change, grow, and learn from your losses.

That, of course, is not necessarily easy. In a favorite *Peanuts* comic strip Charlie Brown walks away from Lucy after a baseball game, head down, totally dejected.

"Another ball game lost! Good grief!" Charlie moans. "I get tired of losing. Everything I do, I lose!"

"Look at it this way, Charlie Brown," Lucy replies. "We learn more from losing than we do from winning."

"That makes me the smartest person in the world!" replies Charlie.

It's a good thought, but not everyone learns from his losses. A loss doesn't turn into a lesson unless we work hard to make it so. Losing gives us an opportunity to learn, but many people do not seize it. And when they don't, losing *really* hurts.

> Losing gives us an opportunity to learn, but many people do not seize it. And when they don't, losing *really* hurts.

Learning is not easy during down times because it requires us to do things that are not natural. It is hard to smile when we are not happy. It is difficult to positively respond when numb with defeat. It takes discipline to do the right thing when everything is wrong. How can we be emotionally strong when we are emotionally exhausted? How will we face others when we are humiliated? How do we get back up when we are continually knocked down?

I wrote this book to answer these and others questions about learning from losses, because I believe it can help you. My primary goal in life is adding value to people. I hope this book will add value to you, teaching you how to learn from your losses. Most of us need someone to help us figure out how to do that. If that is your desire—to become a learner from losses—you need to change the way you look at losses, cultivate qualities that help you respond to them, and develop the ability to learn from them. I believe you can do that using this road map:

Humility: The Spirit of Learning
Reality: The Foundation of Learning

Responsibility: The First Step of Learning

Improvement: The Focus of Learning

Hope: The Motivation of Learning

Teachability: The Pathway of Learning

Adversity: The Catalyst for Learning

Problems: Opportunities for Learning

Bad Experiences: The Perspective for Learning

Change: The Price of Learning

Maturity: The Value of Learning

Saint Ignatius Loyola, one of the world's greatest educators, once said that we learn only when we are ready to learn. As I have traveled and met leaders around the world, I have observed two things. First, most people are currently experiencing difficult times. The idea for this book actually came to me while on a speaking tour through Asia. I could sense that people were having trouble, and I wanted to find a way to help them navigate through difficult waters. Second, I've never experienced a time like the present, when so many people are open not only to learning but also to reexamining their values and priorities. If you see things the right way, losses are opportunities to change and improve.

It is probable that you are at a place in your life where you have suffered some losses and are now ready to learn. Emmet Fox said that difficulties come to you at the right time to help you grow and move forward by overcoming them. "The only real misfortune," he observed, "the only real tragedy, comes when we suffer without learning the lesson."

Let's try to learn some of these lessons together so we can say, "Sometimes You Win, Sometimes You Learn."

2

Humility: The Spirit of Learning

Have you noticed how easily some people bounce back from losses? They learn from them and become even better than they were before! Meanwhile, others seem to fail, fall, and never get back up again. After they experience something negative, you can actually see the downward spiral starting. And no matter how much you want to help them, you can't. They just don't learn from their mistakes.

What is the difference between these two kinds of people? I believe it isn't due to timing, social status, the degree of adversity, or anything else outside of their control. The difference is on the inside. It's the spirit of an individual. Those who profit from adversity possess a spirit of humility and are therefore inclined to make the necessary changes needed to learn from their mistakes, failures, and losses. They stand in stark contrast to prideful people who are unwilling to allow adversity to be their teacher and as a result fail to learn.

Pride Goes before a Fall

Everyone experiences adversity. Some people are made humble by it. Others are made hard. And they carry that spirit with them everywhere they go. For those who allow themselves to become hard, that's tragic because it's very difficult for a hard person to learn anything.

> "Pride is concerned about who's right. Humility is concerned about what's right."
> —*Ezra Taft Benton*

Ezra Taft Benton observed, "Pride is concerned about who's right. Humility is concerned about what's right." That's a pretty accurate description. Pride causes people to justify themselves, even when they know they're wrong. And that's just the start! Take a look at the negative impact pride can have on a person:

- **Blame:** Instead of taking responsibility, prideful people blame others. They believe that someone else is at fault whenever things are not working out for them.
- **Denial:** Instead of being objective and realistic, they don't face reality. The prideful leader of a business will choose to ignore what is obvious to everyone else. The prideful member of a dysfunctional family will rationalize his and others' behavior.
- **Closed Mindedness:** Instead of being open-minded and receptive, prideful people are defensive and opposed to new ideas. They say, "This is the way we've always done it," and they have little interest in innovation or improvement.
- **Rigidity:** Instead of being flexible, prideful people are rigid. They say, "We do it my way or I'm out of here." The ghosts of their past, even their past successes, haunt them and hold them back.

- **Insecurity:** Prideful people inflate themselves and deflate others because they are insecure. They take credit for successes and give others the blame. When insecure people are in positions of leadership, instead of fostering team spirit they create low morale and drive away their best people.
- **Isolation:** Instead of being connected, prideful people find themselves out of touch—with themselves, their families, their community, their clients and customers. Pride makes people think it's all about them when really it's all about others.

Do any of those descriptions apply to you? I'm sorry to say that in my formative years of leadership, I did not possess the humility needed to fill me with the spirit of learning. In fact, I was just the opposite: I was prideful, I was competitive, and I always wanted to win. And when I won, I was insufferable. If I beat someone, I told him I won. And I told everyone he knew that I had won. I put everyone on edge. What's worse is that I wasn't even aware of it. I didn't realize how unteachable I was until my friends gave me the gift of a T-shirt that read, "It's hard to be humble when you're as great as I am." Everyone laughed as they presented it to me, but internally I suspected they were trying to speak truth into my life.

Later I went to one of the presenters and asked if I really was that way.

"Yes," she said, "that's who you are. But we love you and know you can change."

That opened my eyes. Her kind words connected with me and convicted me. And I decided to try to change my attitude from expert to learner.

That decision took a long time to implement—two or three years. Arrogant people don't get humble quickly. But it was the beginning of a change in me, a desire to embrace a humility that makes learning possible. I'm still confident, but I work every day to keep that confidence from becoming a barrier to my ability to learn.

You may already be a humble person who possesses the spirit of learning. If so, that's fantastic. But if you don't, here's the good news: you can change. If I did, then you can, too. If you're not sure where you stand in regard to humility—if your friends haven't given you the T-shirt—then perhaps this can help you. Kirk Hanson, university professor and executive director of the Markkula Center for Applied Ethics at Santa Clara University, offers a list of characteristics exhibited by unteachable leaders. He says these characteristics are often the Achilles' heel of leaders. I believe they also apply to everyone who does not possess the spirit of learning. I've altered his points slightly, stating them as questions so that you can ask yourself which apply to you.

- Do you tend to believe you know it all?
- Do you tend to think you should be in charge?
- Do you sometimes believe the rules don't apply to you?
- Do you believe you shouldn't fail?
- Do you tend to believe you get things done all by yourself?
- Do you believe you are better than others with less talent or status?
- Do you think you are as important as or more important than the organization?

> Remember, it's the finish, not the start, that counts the most in life.

If you answer yes to many of these questions, you may not possess the spirit of learning. Please don't be discouraged. If you have gotten off to a bad start, don't worry. You can change. Remember, it's the finish, not the start, that counts the most in life.

The Good Become the Very Best Due to Humility

People with a lot of talent often perform at a high level, but the greatest—the absolute best of the best—achieve the highest heights because they possess the spirit of learning. I was reminded of this recently when I learned about a story from the early life of one of my heroes: John Wooden. The former UCLA basketball coach is a legend. He's won every award and received every accolade in his profession. He was the first person named to the Basketball Hall of Fame as both a player and a coach.[1]

Wooden was highly talented—so talented, in fact, that he was in danger of being prideful and unteachable. Growing up, he was always the best player on his team, and he went on to lead his high school team to three state championships. But he was fortunate to learn a lesson early on that helped him to develop a spirit of humility. Wooden explained,

> I had forgotten my uniform and did not want to run the mile or so back to our farm to retrieve it before that afternoon's basketball game. Besides, I was the best player on our team—I was sure there was no way Coach was going to bench me. I was wrong.
>
> When it came clear that I would not be allowed to play without the uniform, I talked a teammate into going home to fetch it for me. After all, I was the star, right? Why shouldn't I be allowed to ask a favor or two from the benchwarmers? With that attitude, it's no wonder that the game started without me in

it. When I tried to reason with Coach, pleading with him to let me play because it was clear we were outmatched with our new starting lineup, he told me very simply, "Johnny, there are some things more important than winning."

Some things *more important than winning?* Not many coaches could convince a thirteen-year-old boy to believe that. But as I sat miserably on the bench, watching my team fall farther and farther behind, I started to realize that maybe Coach Warriner was right. Maybe I did need to be taken down a notch or two. As I grew up and that experience stayed with me, I really came to appreciate its significance. The life lessons in responsibility and humility that I needed to learn trumped a hatch mark in the loss column of a grade school-league record book. And at the start of the second half, Coach let me in the game.[2]

As a boy of thirteen, Wooden possessed all of the qualities Kirk Hanson says arrogant leaders possess. He thought he was better than others, that he didn't have to play under the same rules as everyone else, that the team couldn't do without him, that he *was* the team. Fortunately, he had a coach who believed there are things more important than winning, such as learning. And fortunately for Wooden, he learned the lesson early in life.

I believe that's one of the key things that made him great. That lesson in humility influenced Wooden in his life and coaching and made him a lifetime learner. His spirit of learning allowed him to ask questions that many coaches were unwilling to ask. It compelled him to make changes others were unwilling to make. It inspired him to hold on to values that others were tempted to compromise. It empowered him to model graciousness in victory that others rarely do. It's the reason he wanted to be remembered, not for his championships, but as someone who did his best to teach his players about the important things in life.

How the Right Spirit Helps You Learn

John Wooden understood that sometimes you win, sometimes you learn—but only when you possess a humble spirit. Humility is foundational to all people who learn from their wins and losses. It is a key to success at the highest level.

What? you may be thinking. *I disagree! I can name a dozen people who've achieved big things with arrogant attitudes.* So can I. But what *might* they have achieved had they possessed the spirit of learning? Perhaps they would have been even greater. Humility opens the door to learning and to ever higher levels of achievement. Here's why:

1. Humility Allows Us to Possess a True Perspective of Ourselves and Life

Author and business consultant Ken Blanchard says, "Humility does not mean you think less of yourself. It means you think of yourself less." When we are focused too much on ourselves, we lose perspective. Humil-

> "Humility does not mean you think less of yourself. It means you think of yourself less."
> —Ken Blanchard

ity allows us to regain perspective and see the big picture. It makes us realize that while we may be *in* the picture, we are not the *entire* picture.

I've had the privilege on occasion to spend time with Billy Graham. His accomplishments as a religious leader are legendary. That could make a person lose perspective, yet it doesn't seem to have affected him. What has always stood out to me above his accomplishments is his humility. His spirit is typified by an incident that once occurred on an elevator. Another person recognized him, and asked, "You're Billy Graham, aren't you?"

"Yes," Graham replied.

"Well," the man said, "you are truly a great man."

"No, I'm not a great man," responded Graham. "I just have a great message."

When we possess a spirit of pride rather than humility, it clouds our view of ourselves and the world around us. Pioneering psychiatrist Carl Jung said, "Through pride we are ever deceiving ourselves. But deep down below the surface of the average conscience a still, small voice says to us, 'Something is out of tune.'"

When lack of humility makes us "out of tune" within ourselves, the world gets out of focus. We lose perspective and have difficulty learning. How can we discover our shortcomings or the things we need to learn when we can't *see* them?

> "Show me a guy who is afraid to look bad, and I'll show you a guy you can beat every time."
> —*Lou Brock*

Humility opens our eyes and broadens our view. Because we aren't focused on justifying ourselves or looking good, we have better judgment. Baseball great Lou Brock said, "Show me a guy who is afraid to look bad, and I'll show you a guy you can beat every time." Why? Because his eyes are closed to everything around him.

An accurate view of ourselves is difficult to obtain and even harder to keep. Humility helps. John Wooden understood this, and he worked to help his players keep a humble perspective. He didn't want them to get tripped up by either criticism or praise. He knew that whether it was deserved or undeserved, they would always hate the criticism and love the praise.

"Your strength as an individual," Wooden used to tell them, "depends on how you respond to both criticism and praise. If you let either one have any special effect on you, it's going to hurt us.... You have little control over what criticism or praise outsiders send your way. Take it all with a grain of salt. Let your opponent get all caught up in other people's opinions. But don't you do it."[3]

Humility fosters an agenda of seeing things as they really are, of learning, and of the desire to improve. Where pride fosters close-mindedness and always seeks to justify itself, humility fosters open-mindedness and a desire to improve. Humility puts things in perspective, and if we let it, it also helps us to have a better sense of humor.

Winston Churchill, one of Great Britain's greatest prime ministers, was once asked, "Doesn't it thrill you to know that every time you make a speech, the hall is packed to overflowing?"

"It's quite flattering," replied the statesman. "But whenever I feel that way, I always remember that if instead of making a political speech I was being hanged, the crowd would be twice as big."[4]

2. Humility Enables Us to Learn and Grow in the Face of Losses

When people are humble enough to have a clear and realistic view of themselves, their vision is usually also clear and realistic when they face their mistakes, failures, and other losses. That ability to see clearly sets them up to learn and grow. Success lies not in eliminating our troubles and mistakes but in growing through and

> Success lies not in eliminating our troubles and mistakes but in growing through and with them.

with them. Elbert Hubbard described the opposite when he said, "A failure is a man who has blundered but is not able to cash in on the experience."

How does a humble person learn from mistakes? By pausing and reflecting. I strongly believe that experience isn't the best teacher; evaluated experience is. I learned this lesson from the Book of Ecclesiastes, which states, "In the day of prosperity be joyful, but in the day of adversity consider."[5] It's believed that Ecclesiastes was written by King Solomon of Israel, said to be the wisest man who ever lived. When someone with that kind of wisdom speaks, we'd all do well to listen.

> Wisely humble people are never afraid to admit they were wrong. When they do it's like saying they're wiser today than they were yesterday.

Wisely humble people are never afraid to admit they were wrong. When they do it's like saying they're wiser today than they were yesterday. And of course there are other side benefits. As the great American novelist Mark Twain quipped, "Always acknowledge a fault frankly. This will throw those in authority off their guard and give you an opportunity to commit more."

Mistakes can often be our best teachers. If we are willing to admit them and learn from them, we gain in knowledge and wisdom. We can do so if every time we take time to reflect on them by asking:

What went wrong?
When did it go wrong?
Where did it go wrong?
Why did it go wrong?
How did I contribute to making it go wrong?
What can I learn from this experience?
How will I apply what I've learned in the future?

Asking such questions can be a slow and uncomfortable process, especially for action-oriented people. But it always pays off. Humanity is filled with mistakes. Humility allows us to learn from them.

3. Humility Allows Us to Let Go of Perfection and Keep Trying

My grandson John, the son of my son Joel and his wife Liz, is a wonderful child. (I'd say that even if he weren't my grandchild!) He's very smart, but he also tends to be a bit serious and perfectionistic. To help him with this, his parents bought him a book entitled *Mistakes That Worked* by Charlotte Foltz Jones. They read through it together, and it helps him to understand that he doesn't need to be perfect to be successful.

In the book, Jones writes,

> Call them accidents. Call them mistakes. Even serendipity.
>
> If the truth were known, we might be amazed by the number of great inventions and discoveries that were accidental, unplanned and unintentional.
>
> The inventors mentioned in this book were not only smart, but also alert. It is easy to fail and then abandon the whole idea. It's more difficult to fail, but then recognize another use for the failure....
>
> The inventors and discoverers mentioned in this book should teach all of us the lesson stated best by Bertolt Brecht in 1930: "Intelligence is not to make no mistakes. But quickly to see how to make them good." [6]

One of John's favorite stories in the book is about pharmacist John Pemberton of Atlanta, Georgia. In 1886, the pharmacist wanted to develop a new remedy for prospective customers. He had already invented "French Wine Coca—The Ideal Nerve Tonic, Health Restorer and Stimulant," "Lemon and Orange Elixir," and "Dr. Pemberton's Indian Queen Magic Hair Dye." This time he created a new medicine to relieve exhaustion, aid the nervous, and soothe headaches.

Pemberton was happy with his product, a syrup that he mixed with water and served chilled. But then a happy accident occurred. Pemberton's assistant accidentally mixed the concoction with soda water. The drink was transformed. Pemberton wasn't too proud to admit that his original vision for the drink was inferior to his assistant's creation, and as a result, he decided not to sell it as a medicine, but instead as a fountain drink. He named it Coca-Cola.[7] Today, Coca-Cola is the most popular soft drink in the world.

4. Humility Allows Us to Make the Most Out of Our Mistakes

That brings us to the final way that a humble spirit of learning helps us—by allowing us to make the most out of our mistakes and failures. Novelist Mark Twain was once asked to name the greatest of all inventors. His reply: "Accidents." His answer is clever, but it also reveals a great truth. When we're humble, we are open to seeing our mistakes as possibilities for innovation and success.

> Mark Twain was once asked to name the greatest of all inventors. His reply: "Accidents."

History is filled with accounts of scientists and inventors who made mistakes that turned into great discoveries. In 1839, Charles Goodyear was conducting experiments with rubber. The substance, derived from tree sap, had been known for centuries. People had tried to put it to practical use, but when hot it melted and when cold it shattered. Goodyear tried mixing it with various substances, but none transformed it into a usable substance. Then one day he accidently dropped some rubber mixed with sulfur on a hot kitchen stove. The heat made the rubber firm and flexible. Even cold air didn't make it brittle. Goodyear's mistake helped him transform rubber into the substance used in so many products and industries today.[8]

Cellophane is another substance discovered by accident. Swiss textile engineer Jacques Brandenberger wanted to develop a waterproof cloth after seeing a bottle of wine spilled on a tablecloth. The coating he created was too stiff and brittle to be practical. But Brandenberger discovered that the transparent film peeled off of the fabric in whole sheets. By 1908 he developed a machine that could produce those sheets.[9]

Penicillin was also the result of a mistake. When researcher Alexander Fleming accidentally introduced mold into the flu culture in one of his petri dishes in 1928, he didn't deride his sloppy efforts. He studied the results. He isolated and identified the mold, which led to the creation of the vaccine that has saved countless lives.

The cooking power of microwaves was discovered when an engineer mistakenly melted a chocolate bar in his pocket using them. Teflon was discovered when a researcher working on refrigerants left out a sample overnight by mistake. Post-it notes were developed because of a mistake developing a new adhesive.

If you bring the right spirit to your work, you can turn a mistake into an opportunity. Success and fame don't always come to the most talented people. Sometimes they come to the person who can turn adversity into advantage. Or, as John Kenneth Galbraith says, "If all else fails, immortality can always be assured by spectacular error."

> "If all else fails, immortality can always be assured by spectacular error."
> —John Kenneth Galbraith

A Portrait of Humility

I love the story of humility contained in the life of the person who has been called an American Renaissance man. His first love was art, and he grew up wanting to be a painter. But he had a learner's mind-set and a humble spirit, which fed his curious mind and made his interests vary widely. At Yale he studied religious philosophy, mathematics, and science, graduating at age nineteen. Having finished his formal education, his parents insisted that he become a bookseller's apprentice. But his primary passion was painting. He tried to convince his parents to allow him to go abroad to train as an artist. After a year, they finally relented, sending him to England to study painting. He excelled. A plaster sculpture he created won a gold medal at the Adelphi Society of Arts, and a large canvas he painted received critical acclaim at the Royal Academy.

Upon his return to the United States, he opened a studio in Boston and became a respected painter traveling from town to town, seeking commissions to paint portraits. While in Concord, New Hampshire, he met a girl whom he wrote to tell his parents about in a letter dated August 20, 1816:

> My Dear Parents,
>
> I write you a few lines just to say I am well and very indus-
> trious, next day after to-morrow I shall have rec.'d 100 dollars,
> which I think is pretty well for 3 weeks, I shall probably stay
> here a fortnight from yesterday; I have other attractions beside
> money in this place; do you know the Walkers of this place,
> Chas. Walker the son of Judge W. has two daughters, the eldest
> very beautiful, amiable, and of an excellent disposition....I
> may flatter myself but I think I might be a successful suitor;

you will perhaps think me a terrible harum scarum fellow, to be continually falling in love in this way, but I have a dread of being an old bachelor and I am *25* years of age; there is still no need of hurry the young lady is but *16*.[10]

He was madly in love. Less than a month later, he followed up the first letter to his parents with an update. He wrote,

Every thing is successful beyond my most sanguine expectations, the more I know her the more amiable she appears, she is very beautiful, and yet no coquetry, she is modest quite to diffidence and yet frank and open hearted, whenever I have enquired concerning her I have invariably heard the same character of remarkably amiable, modest, and of a sweet disposition. When you learn that this is the case, I think you will not accuse me of being hasty in bringing the affair to a crisis. I ventured to tell her my whole heart, and I found instead of obscure and ambiguous answers, which some would have given to tantalize & pain one, she frankly but modestly and timidly, told me it was mutual, suffice it to say we are engaged; . . . never was a human being so blest as I am, and yet what an ungrateful wretch have I been; Pray for me that I may have a grateful heart for I deserve nothing but adversity, and yet have the most unbounded prosperity.[11]

She waited for him for two years, and on September 29, 1818, they were married. Nearly a year later, they had their first child, a girl.

As their family grew, so did his success as a painter. He painted important people such as inventor Eli Whitney, Yale president Jeremiah Day, writer and lexicographer Noah Webster, the Marquis de

Lafayette, and United States president James Monroe. Meanwhile he still cultivated his love for invention and innovation. He and his brother developed a water pump for fire engines, which they patented but could not make profitable. He also invented a marble-cutting machine to carve sculptures, but was unable to patent it.

He seemed to be well on his way. Then in 1825, while he was working on a painting in New York, he received a letter from his father saying that his wife was ill. The man rushed home, but by the time he got there, his wife had already died. He was devastated by her loss. What made it even worse was that by the time he got home, she had already been buried. He hadn't even been able to attend the funeral.

The man's name was Samuel F. B. Morse. He recovered from his grief over his wife's death, but his frustration over the slow speed of communication stayed with him. As a result, he began learning about electricity and electromagnetism. And in 1832, he conceived of a device capable of sending messages by wire over long distances. He also began formulating a code comprised of dots and dashes that could be used to communicate.

The early 1800s was a time of experimentation and rapid advances in electricity. Morse humbly learned about others' advances and studied their inventions. He modified his designs several times. By 1838, he was demonstrating his communication device, which he called the telegraph. The invention of that device, along with the code that carries his name, is what Morse became known for. It brought the world into the modern era of communication. Where once it took days, weeks, or months to communicate with others far away, thanks to Morse it took minutes. The technology changed the world.

Morse received many honors from his invention of the telegraph, but he was always very humble about it. He once said, "I have made a valuable application of electricity not because I was superior to other men but solely because God, who meant it for mankind, must reveal it to someone and He was pleased to reveal it to me."[12] With that attitude, no wonder he was able to bounce back from his losses, learn, and grow. He possessed the spirit of learning. And we would do well to obtain it too.

> "The life of every man is a diary in which he means to write one story, and writes another; and his humblest hour is when he compares the volume as it is with what he vowed to make it."
> —J. M. Barrie

Novelist J. M. Barrie observed, "The life of every man is a diary in which he means to write one story and writes another; and his humblest hour is when he compares the volume as it is with what he vowed to make it." That has been true for me. In many ways, I've fallen short of what I would have liked to do and be. However, in the hour when we compare what we desired to do with what we have actually done, if we are humble and open to the lessons life offers to teach us, we increase the odds of our success. And knowing that we have tried our best, perhaps we will be content with what we have been able to become and to accomplish.

3

Reality: The Foundation of Learning

Charlene Schiff was born into a comfortable, loving family in the small town of Horochow, Poland. She had a good childhood. Her father was a philosophy professor at a nearby university, who loved her and was patient with her, even when she did wrong. Once when her mother was working to paint some rooms in their house, Charlene impulsively took the paintbrush and painted the family's piano. Her father didn't yell at her. He did discipline her, but he also took into consideration that she was immediately repentant. And he used the incident to teach her how important it was not to destroy other people's property.

Charlene's mother was a teacher, but she gave up her teaching career to raise Charlene and her older sister, Tia. Her mother doted on her, buying her clothes and toys and encouraging her daily. She had a wonderful life.

An Ugly Reality Emerges

But then things began to change for Charlene. In 1939, when Charlene was ten, Poland was invaded by Germany and the Soviet Union and divided between them. Horochow, where Charlene lived, was annexed by the Soviets. Despite that, life didn't change much for her family at that time. But in 1941 it did. That was when Hitler decided to take over all of Poland and his troops entered the city. Immediately, Charlene's beloved father was dragged off by the Nazis. She never saw him again. Soon Charlene, her mother, and her sister were relocated to a Jewish ghetto, being forced to share a single room with three other families. Charlene was only eleven.

Charlene's mother was subjected to forced labor. And the girls were sometimes made to work as well. There was little food, and it was a struggle to survive. But Charlene's mother came up with a plan. She began looking for people in the countryside who might be willing to take them in and hide them. She found a farmer who agreed to take one of them. It was decided that it would be Charlene's sister, who was five years older than she was. Another farmer said he would take Charlene and her mother.

"One day, in 1942, I guess it was early summer, I don't remember dates, but I remember we got up and I said good-bye to my terrific big sister," recounted Charlene. "Now when we didn't hear for a few days anything, that meant that she arrived in good shape and everything was going according to plan, my mother came home from work and she told me to put on my best clothes and shoes and to take an extra set with me and that we would leave the ghetto that evening."[1]

The ghetto where they were living was bounded on three sides by fences and on the fourth side by a river. Late that night under the cloak of darkness, they left their room and made their way to the river. They waded in. But before they could cross, they heard shots. On the bank of the river, soldiers waited. "We can see you, Jew!" they shouted. Others had the same idea as Charlene and her mother. They also wished to escape. Many who were hiding stood up and raised their hands to surrender. When they did, they were promptly shot.[2]

Charlene and her mother huddled among the reeds. The water was up to the young girl's neck. Her mother kept her quiet and fed her soggy bread. They stayed in the river for four days! On the morning of the last day, Charlene awoke and her mother was gone.

A Child All Alone

The reality of her situation was dire. At age eleven, she was all alone living in a hostile land where she would be hunted down and killed like an animal. "I felt like screaming but I knew I had to keep quiet," Charlene recalled.[3]

With the soldiers finally gone, Charlene made her way to the farm where they had promised to hide her and her mother. Instead of a warm welcome, she was told she could spend the day in the barn but that when it got dark she had to leave or the farmer would turn her in to the Nazis.

At first, Charlene would not face the reality of her situation. She said, "I lived like an animal, going from forest to forest, in search of my mother. I could not allow myself to think that I would never find my mother. I had to find my mother. Where was I going to go, what was I going to eat, who would take care of me?"[4]

The reality of such an overwhelming situation causes some people to crumble, others to adapt and learn what they must to survive. Charlene did the latter. The girl who grew up in town totally dependent on her mother learned to survive on her own in the woods. Occasionally she stumbled across other Jews hiding from the authorities. Once she came across a small group of men, women, and a baby, who had escaped their ghettos. When the group was discovered by local children, they and Charlene hid in a nearby haystack. But local villagers used pitchforks to jab the haystack, killing all but Charlene.

Another time when Charlene was returning to her sleeping place after scrounging for food, a girl of about eighteen befriended her and offered to help her. They agreed to meet the next morning. But during the night Charlene had a bad feeling about the girl. The next day, she hid herself high in a tree and waited. Sure enough, the girl showed up, this time with her brother. As Charlene listened, she learned that the two had planned to rob her and turn her over to the authorities for a reward.[5]

Charlene did experience a few moments of kindness during those years. Once she was discovered sleeping in a barn by a hired farm girl, who brought her food and clothing. "It took a long time to sink in," Charlene remembered. "I had [finally] been treated like a human being, with kindness and generosity. I had forgotten how that felt." The girl fed Charlene for almost two weeks. But then one day two policemen arrived at the farm and shot the farm girl, whom they said was a Jew.[6]

"I spent two years in the woods alone," recounted Charlene. "I slept during the day in a little grave I'd dug, and at night I would crawl out and search for something—anything—to eat. I became very ill."[7]

In 1944, Charlene was discovered by Soviet troops who literally stepped on her as she lay in her hiding place. They took her to a hospital, where she was slowly nursed back to health. Her goal was to make it to the United States, where other family members had gone before the war. Finally in 1948, she made the journey there. Three years later she was married.

Charlene didn't want to talk about her experiences and kept them to herself for years. But eventually her husband Ed convinced her that she needed to tell her story to others. "You have a mandate and an obligation to six million martyrs," he said.[8] Now she shares her story and the reality she had to face in hopes that it will also teach others.

"I also want to send a message of hope to the young people of today," said Charlene. "I'm an optimist, and I feel that younger generations will learn from the mistakes that my generation made and will fight indifference and injustice."[9]

Build on a Good Foundation

If we want to succeed in life and to learn from our losses, we must be able to face reality and use it to create a foundation for growth. That can be very difficult. People who face horrific experiences, as Charlene Schiff did, can be crushed by them. But even losses less cata-strophic than hers can tempt us to avoid reality. We may blame other people for our circumstances. We may rationalize or make excuses. Or we may retreat into our own little world, like this man in one of my favorite "reality" stories. He had been an insomniac for thirty years, and finally he decided to see a psychiatrist.

"Why can't you sleep at night?" the doctor asked.

"Because I'm trying to solve the world's problems," the man responded.

The psychiatrist pressed further, "Do you ever solve them?"

"Almost every time," replied the patient earnestly.

"Then why can't you sleep?" the psychiatrist asked.

"Well Doctor, I think it's those big ticker tape parades they have in my honor that keep me up."

As much as an escape from reality might give us temporary relief from our problems, the truth is it's easier to go from failure to suc-cess than it is from excuses to suc-cess. When we lose sight of reality we quickly lose our way. We cannot create positive change in our lives if we are

> It's easier to go from failure to success than it is from excuses to success.

confused about what's really happening. You can't improve yourself if you're kidding yourself.

Three Realities of Life

Everyone's reality is different. However, there are some realities that are true for all of life.

1. Life Is Difficult

Somehow people seem to believe that life is supposed to be easy. This is particularly a problem in America today. We expect a smooth easy road to success. We expect our lives to be hassle free. We expect the government to solve our problems. We expect to get the prize without having to pay the price. That is not reality! Life is hard.

In *Life's Greatest Lessons*, Hal Urban writes,

> Once we accept the fact that life is hard, we begin to grow. We begin to understand that every problem is also an opportunity. It is then that we dig down and discover what we're made of. We begin to accept the challenges of life. Instead of letting our hardships defeat us, we welcome them as a test of character. We use them as a means of rising to the occasion.
>
> At the same time, we need to understand that society bombards us daily with messages that are quite the opposite. To begin with, technology has provided us with push-button living. We can open the garage door, cook dinner, wash the dishes, record our favorite TV program, and pay our bills by simply pushing the right buttons. In addition, we're told over and over that there's a quick and easy way to do just about everything.

Within just the past few days, I've read or heard that you can lose a hundred pounds, learn to speak a foreign language fluently, become a hot new radio personality, get a contractor's license, and make a million dollars in real estate. You can do all of these in a matter of days, and with little or no effort. And pigs can fly.

Those ads are all around us because the people in advertising and marketing have a good understanding of human behavior. They know that most people *don't* accept life as hard and will continue to look for the quick and easy way instead.[10]

There is no quick and easy way. Nothing worth having in life comes without effort. That is why psychiatrist M. Scott Peck begins his book *The Road Less Traveled* with the words, "Life is difficult." He wants to set the stage for everything else he communicates in the book. If we don't understand and accept the truth that life is difficult, then we set ourselves up for failure and we won't learn.

2. Life Is Difficult for Everyone

Even if we are willing to concede that life is difficult for most people, deep down inside many of us secretly hope somehow that this truth won't apply to us. I'm sorry to say it isn't so. No one escapes life's problems, failures, and losses. If we are to make progress, we must do so through life's difficulties. Or as poet Ralph Waldo Emerson stated it, "The walking of Man is falling forwards."

> "The walking of Man is falling forwards."
> —*Ralph Waldo Emerson*

Life isn't easy and it isn't fair. I've had unfair things happen to me. I bet you have, too. I've made mistakes, made a fool of myself, hurt

people I've loved, and experienced crushing disappointments. I bet
you have, too. We cannot avoid life's difficulties. We shouldn't even
try. Why? Because the people who succeed in life don't try to escape
pain, loss, or unfairness. They just learn to face those things, accept
them, and move ahead in the face of them. That's my goal. It should
also be yours.

3. Life Is More Difficult for Some Than for Others

In a favorite *Peanuts* comic strip, the woeful Charlie Brown pours
his heart out to Lucy, who is positioned in her five-cents psychiatric
booth. When he tells her that he's confused about life and where he's
going, she says. "Life is like a deck chair. On the cruise ship of life,
some people place their chairs facing the rear of the ship so they can
see where they've been. Other people face their chairs forward; they
want to see where they're going." Then Lucy asks, "Which way is your
deck chair facing?"

Charlie's reply: "I've never been able to get one unfolded."

Let's face it: life is more difficult for some than it is for others. The
playing field is not level. You may have faced more and greater difficulties in life than I have. You may have faced fewer. Your life right
now may feel like clear sailing. Or it may feel like rough waters. And
comparing our lives to others ultimately isn't that productive. Life isn't
fair, and we shouldn't expect it to be. The sooner we face that reality,
the better we are going to be at facing whatever is coming toward us.

Don't Make Life Harder for Yourself

Your life is probably plenty difficult already. The reality is that you
will have to deal with those difficulties already no matter what. One

of the keys to winning is to not make things even harder for yourself, which is, unfortunately, what many people seem to do.

To help you with this reality, I want to point out the top five ways people make life harder for themselves so that you can avoid these pitfalls.

1. Life Is More Difficult for Those Who Stop Growing and Learning

As you know, some people never make the intentional effort to grow. Some think they will grow automatically. Others don't value growth and hope to progress in life without pursuing it. For such people, life is more difficult than it would be if they were dedicating themselves to continual improvement.

People who won't grow are like the peers of the great scientist Galileo, who tried to convince them to believe what he was learning about physics. They laughed at him and refused to acknowledge his discoveries, saying that his theories could not be true because they contradicted the teachings of Aristotle.

In one instance, Galileo decided to give them a demonstration that would provide them with clear evidence of one of his observations: that two objects of different mass dropped together from the same height would reach the ground at the same time. On the day of the demonstration, the scientist climbed to the top of the leaning tower of Pisa. As the crowd below watched, he let drop together a ten-pound shot and a one-pound shot. They landed simultaneously. There could be no doubt that Galileo's theory was correct. Yet many still refused to believe it—in spite of the evidence they saw with their own eyes. And they continued teaching the outdated theories of Aristotle. They wanted to hold on to what they had—even though it was wrong—rather than change and grow.

While some people experience greater difficulties in life because they refuse to grow, there are additional kinds of people who create difficulties for themselves: those who become satisfied with their gains and start to plateau.

A few years ago Margaret and I visited the Nobel Museum in Stockholm, Sweden. We spent hours listening to lectures and reading about people who have made a difference in so many lives. Our tour guide shared something with us that day that surprised us. He said very few of the Nobel Prize winners ever did anything significant after they had been recognized for their achievements. I found it hard to believe, but after doing some research I concluded that he was correct. Daniel McFadden, who received the Nobel Prize for Economics in 2000, said, "If you're not careful, the Nobel Prize is a career-ender. If I allowed myself to slip into it, I'd spend all my time going around cutting ribbons." Literature winner T. S. Eliot stated it even more strongly: "The Nobel is a ticket to one's own funeral. No one has ever done anything after he got it."

Success can have a way of distorting our view of reality. It can make us think we are better than we really are. It can lure us into believing we have little left to learn. It can convince us that we should no longer expect to face and overcome failure. These are dangerous concepts to anyone who wants to keep improving.

How do we fight such ideas? By facing reality. Successful coaches understand the importance of honest and realistic evaluation. In football, that means spending time in the film room grading the performance of the team. My friend Jim Tressel, former coach at Ohio State, says, "Grade the plays the same, win or lose." Why? Because there is a tendency to not be as objective grading plays when you win as when you lose.

> "Grade the plays the same, win or lose."
> —Jim Tressel

Winning causes people to relax and enjoy the spoils of victory. Do that and you just may coast your way to failure.

2. Life Is More Difficult for Those Who Don't Think Effectively

One of the most striking things that separate people who are successful from those who aren't is the way they think. I feel so strongly about this I wrote a book about it called *How Successful People Think*. People who get ahead think differently than those who don't. They have reasons for doing what they do, and they are continually thinking about what they're doing, why they're doing it, and how they can improve.

That doesn't mean that good thinkers always succeed. No, they make mistakes just like everyone else. But they don't keep making the *same* mistakes repeatedly. And that makes a great difference in their lives. Frank Gaines, who was the mayor of Berkeley, California, from 1939 to 1943, explained,

> It never bothers me for people to make a mistake if they had a reason for what they did. If they can tell me, "I thought this and reasoned so, and came to that decision," if they obviously went through a reasonable thought process to get where they did, even if it didn't turn out right, that's OK. The ones you want to watch out for are those who can't even tell you why they did what they did.

I have to admit, even though I place a high value on good thinking, I've often been guilty of not thinking things through as I should. A prime example of that occurred during the 1980s, when I was the lead pastor of a church in San Diego, California. Back then many pastors like me had heard about the astonishing growth a congregation in Seoul, South Korea, was experiencing by starting small groups that met all around their city. I traveled to Korea to learn about it firsthand. My time there was very inspirational—so much so that I went back home and shared the small-group story with the people of my congregation. They were inspired.

A few weeks later in my enthusiasm I cast vision to start thirty small groups within the coming year. The people responded wholeheartedly, and we launched our small-group program. I wish I could tell you that it was wildly successful, but it wasn't. Within only a few months, we could tell that it wasn't working. By the end of the year, instead of having thirty small groups, we had only three! What happened? I had failed to train enough small group leaders to lead the groups. Any group that was started without a trained leader fizzled out and disbanded.

Today the lesson seems clear and simple to me: an organization can sustain only as many groups as it has trained leaders to lead them. That's the reality. Back then I hadn't thought it through, but I quickly learned my lesson. For the next two years we trained hundreds of leaders, and then we relaunched our small-group program again. That second time it was successful.

We often make life harder for ourselves when we fail to think. A joke I came across years ago describes how many people make a bad situation worse by failing to think things through. It describes the strategies people use when they discover they are riding a dead horse. They try the following:

- Buying a stronger whip
- Changing riders
- Saying things like, "This is the way we've always ridden this horse"

- Appointing a committee to study the horse
- Arranging a visit to other sites to see how they ride horses
- Changing the by-laws to specify that "horses shall not die"
- Harnessing several dead horses together for increased speed
- Declaring that "no horse is too dead to ride"
- Providing additional funding to increase the horse's performance
- Purchasing a product to revitalize the dead horse
- Forming a quality circle to find uses for dead horses
- Revisiting the performance requirement for horses
- Promoting the dead horse to a supervisory position[11]

These ridiculous practices were cited as being used in business, but we can do such things in any area of our lives when we don't use our heads. Life is filled with plenty of disappointments and heartaches without our adding to the problem.

3. Life Is More Difficult for Those Who Don't Face Reality

Perhaps the people who have the hardest time in life are the ones who refuse to face reality. Author and speaker Denis Waitley says, "Most people spend their entire lives on a fantasy island called 'Someday I'll.'" In other words, they think, *Someday I'll do this. Someday I'll do that. Someday I'll be rich.* They don't live in the world of reality.

> "Most people spend their entire lives on a fantasy island called 'Someday I'll.'"
> —*Denis Waitley*

They're like the average-looking young woman talking to a priest in the confession booth.

"I'm guilty of the grievous sin of vanity," she admitted to the priest. "Only this morning I looked into my mirror and admired my beauty."

"Is that all, my daughter?" the priest asked, having known her since she was a child.

"Yes, Father," she answered sheepishly.

"Then go in peace," said the priest. "To be mistaken is not to sin."

Roots author Alex Haley observed, "Either you deal with what is the reality, or you can be sure that the reality is going to deal with you." If you want to climb the highest mountain, you can't expect to do it overnight. You can't expect to do it unless you've been trained in how to climb and gotten into physical condition. And if you try to deny reality and make the climb anyway, you're going to end up in trouble.

> "Either you deal with what is the reality, or you can be sure that the reality is going to deal with you."
> —*Alex Haley*

What you do matters. And to be successful, what you do must be based on reality. Journalist Sydney J. Harris observed, "An idealist believes the short run doesn't count. A cynic believes the long run doesn't matter. A realist believes that what is done or left undone in the short run determines the long run."

Life is difficult. But here's the good news: many of the things you desire to do in life are attainable—if you are willing to face reality, know your starting place, count the cost of your goal, and put in the work. Don't let your real situation discourage you. Everyone who got where they are, started where they were.

4. Life Is More Difficult for Those Who Are Slow to Make Proper Adjustments

My older brother, Larry, has been a mentor to me in many areas. He is especially gifted when it comes to business and finance. Often I have heard him say, "People don't cut their losses quickly enough." He has taught me to make my first loss my last loss. I find that difficult to do. Do you? Instead of cutting our losses, we rationalize. We try to defend the decision. We wait to see if it will change and prove us right. Larry advised me to face up to a problem and either fix it or bail out.

The great heavyweight boxer Evander Holyfield said, "Everyone has a plan until they are hit." What did he mean by that? The stress of a difficult situation can make you forget your plan and if you don't handle the situation well, you won't be able to make adjustments. Yet that is exactly what you need to be able to do—make good adjustments.

While it's true that acceptance of a problem does not conquer it, if you face reality you create a foundation making it possible for you to make proper adjustments. And that greatly increases your odds of success.

Advertising executive and friend Linda Kaplan Thaler has been very successful in helping companies brand and market their products. She is the person who came up with the idea for the duck in the Aflac insurance commercials. She has worked on ads for many successful products, but she really loves to represent unsuccessful ones. She says, "I love working on a product that is 'D-listed,' meaning dead." Why? The companies "are desperate so they will let me do anything." Sadly, many people are unwilling to face reality and make adjustments until after something has died. If we want to be successful, we can't wait that long.

5. Life Is More Difficult for Those Who Don't Respond Correctly to Challenges

People who respond correctly to adversity realize that their response to a challenge is what impacts the outcome. They accept and acknowledge the reality of their situation, and then act accordingly. I didn't find that to be easy at first. My natural optimism tends to make me want to ignore a crisis and hope it will go away. That doesn't work. Wishing isn't solving. Denying a problem only makes it worse. So does getting angry and yelling, or taking it out on loved ones. I had to learn to say to myself, "This is the way it is. I have a problem. If I want to solve it, I need to take action. What is the best solution?" When you have a challenge, you can turn lemons into lemonade, or you can let them sour your whole life. It's your choice.

Facing reality, maintaining a confident sense of expectation, and performing at your best may not be easy, but it is possible. And it does make a huge difference in your life. It sets you up to learn, to grow, and to succeed. That's what Jim Lovell did when he was leading the Apollo 13 mission to the moon. When the Saturn rocket that was pushing them toward the lunar surface malfunctioned and they had to abort the mission and try to return safely to Earth, the future looked grim. Lovell calculated that their chances of survival seemed slim. "But you don't put that in your mind," Lovell noted at a forty-year reunion of the mission's remaining astronauts and flight directors. "You don't say how slim they are but rather how you can improve the odds."[12]

Author and business expert Jim Collins says, "There is a sense of exhilaration that comes from facing head-on the hard truths and saying, 'We will never give up. We will never capitulate. It might take a long time, but we will find a way to prevail.'" That's a fantastic way of stating the correct response to challenges. You create opportunities by looking trouble in the eye and performing, not looking away and pretending. If you want to learn, you must build your problem solving, your planning, and your performance on a solid foundation. Reality is the only thing that won't crumble under the weight of those things.

4

Responsibility: The First
Step of Learning

We tend to think of responsibility as something *given* to us by someone who is in a position of authority, such as a parent or an employer. And that is often the case. But responsibility is also something we must be willing to *take*. And after more than forty years leading and mentoring people, I have come to the conclusion that responsibility is the most important ability that a person can possess. Nothing happens to advance our potential until we step up and say, "I am responsible." If you don't take responsibility, you give up control of your life.

> Responsibility is the most important ability that a person can possess.

My friend Truett Cathy, the founder of Chick-fil-A, often says, "If it's to be, it's up to me." That's the right mind-set for winning. Taking responsibility for your life, your actions, your mistakes, and your growth puts you in a place where you are always able to learn and often able to win. In sports, that's called being in the right position.

When players put themselves in the right position, they are able to successfully play. It's not a guarantee that they will make a play or that they will win. However, if they are out of position, it is almost impossible for them to make a play. Miss enough plays, and you lose the game.

Every time we fail, we can choose to put ourselves in the painful but potentially profitable place of taking responsibility so that we can take right actions for our success, or we can avoid the temporary pain of responsibility and make excuses. If we respond right to failure by taking responsibility, we can look at our failure and learn from it. As a result, we won't be as prone to making the same mistake again. However, if we bail out on our responsibility, we don't examine our failures and don't learn from them. As a result, we often experience the same failures and losses repeatedly over time.

A Golden Voice

That's what happened to Ted Williams. No, not the legendary baseball player for the Red Sox, but the man whose image was captured on video at the side of the road and posted on YouTube. You may have seen it. A homeless man stands at a freeway exit, sign in hand, hoping to receive money from passersby. A driver with a video camera stops and says, "Hey, I'm going to make you work for your dollar. Say something with that great radio voice."[1]

The homeless man, wearing an army fatigue jacket, his hair wild and uncut, responds by launching into a well-practiced spiel with a magnificent voice built for radio. In fact, on the streets Ted was known as "Radio," and he always considered his golden voice to be a gift from God.

Ted became famous overnight when the video on YouTube went viral. He appeared on the *Today* show, *Entertainment Tonight*, and *Dr. Phil*. It was a feel-good story that people connected with—homeless man with a talent gets a break. But Ted's story has a lot more to it than that, and it is an illustration in the power of responsibility as the first step of learning.

From Dream to Nightmare

When Ted was ten years old, his mother gave him a Panasonic radio. He listened to it constantly. What captivated him most were the DJs. He listened to them every night, learning their speech patterns, copying their inflections. When he was twelve, he got a tape recorder and microphone for Christmas. Every day he spent hours talking into it, creating his own radio phrases, reading news copy he'd written, rehearsing difficult sentences. He had discovered what he wanted to do with his life: be on radio.

When he turned seventeen, Ted took a step that he hoped would take him closer to his dream. A United States Army recruiter told him he could become a communications specialist. So he dropped out of high school and joined the army. What the recruiter had neglected to mention was that the job required the ability to type, and Ted couldn't. So after finishing basic training, he was assigned to a truck maintenance unit. He was what he called "a mechanic for the South Korea outhouse patrol."[2] It was around that time that Ted started drinking heavily. That, along with other bad behavior, caused him to leave the Army with a dishonorable discharge.

Ted moved to South Carolina and eventually got a job working at a small country radio station, where he began to learn the business and see some success. After a scrape with the law and some jail time, he moved to Columbus, Ohio, and married a woman he'd known in high school. He got a job, and occasionally he worked as an emcee at a concert or nightclub. When a new radio station started in town, he landed a DJ job. "I worked hard," Ted remembers. "I came in early every day to work on my production, recording segments and splicing them together with sound effects."[3] His show started at seven p.m. and he finished at midnight. He added commercial voiceover work to that.

A Dark Road

In time, Ted became the number one DJ in Columbus. But he never stopped drinking—not when it and the bad behavior that often goes with it got him fired. Or when he had to change jobs. Or when his marriage fell apart. Or when he got demoted. He just kept drinking. He also smoked marijuana. Then one day his life went from horrible to worse. Some friends came to visit him and they gave him his first experience with crack cocaine. He was instantly hooked.

Ted says at first "I thought, *I can just smoke on the weekends.* Then, *I can just smoke at night and every weekend, and everything will be fine.*" He continued lying to himself and smoking more and more. "Two months after smoking my first hit of crack, I walked out on my dream job, the only thing I'd ever wanted to do with my life," Ted recalls.[4] He quit so that he could smoke crack all day. And that's what he did. "Within three months of my first smoke, most of what I'd accumulated in my five years at the top was gone."[5]

Ted went from poverty to homelessness. He lived on the streets, sleeping in the woods, on strangers' couches, and in crack houses. He lived a never-ending cycle of addiction, drug abuse, hustling, petty theft, and homelessness punctuated with occasional stints in jail. All the while, he told himself the lie that he was doing okay. But he wasn't. He was slowly killing himself. "Lying to yourself is a hard habit to break," says Ted. "But the truth is, there wasn't nothing glamorous about the life. Nothing fun about spending a few months every year in jail. Nothing positive about never taking showers, having terrible breath, rifling through rain-soaked clothes outside the Salvation Army drop box for something decent to wear. . . . I was nothing more than a broken man desperately hustling for the next fix."[6] That lasted twenty years!

By the time Ted was discovered on that street corner with his sign, he'd been attempting to change his life, but he was having a difficult time finding his way. His whirlwind of fame didn't help. He still hadn't really looked his addiction in the face and taken responsibility for himself. He accepted Dr. Phil's offer for rehab, but he didn't really want to go. He bailed out after only twelve days. Months later after consuming more alcohol and crack, he'd finally had enough.

"I went back to Dr. Phil, hat in hand, humility in heart, and asked for another chance," says Ted. His second chance paid off. "For the first time since I ruined my last chance at radio in 1996, I was clean. I wasn't cured. No addict is ever cured. But for the first time in my life, I felt free."[7] For perhaps the first time in his life he was learning. Why? Because he finally took responsibility for himself and his choices, and that is the first step of learning.

What Happens When We Don't Take Responsibility

The stories of addicts like Ted Williams are sad and always strikingly similar. When Ted lived on the streets, he lied, cheated, and stole to feed his habit. He betrayed the people he loved. He begged for money from his mother so that he could travel home to New York for his father's funeral, and when she sent it, he spent it on crack. He betrayed his wife. He abandoned his children. And he refused to take responsibility for anything.

Ted's story is extreme, but he is not alone in his avoidance of responsibility. People do that all the time, especially when they fail or make mistakes. They just don't want to face up to those things. If we do that long enough, a pattern begins to emerge in our lives:

1. We Develop a Victim Mentality

Twenty years ago, Charles J. Sykes wrote a book entitled *A Nation of Victims* in which he decried the victim mentality that had arisen among people in the United States. In the book's opening pages, he describes an FBI agent who embezzled two thousand dollars and lost it while gambling in Atlantic City. The man was fired, but he won reinstatement after he convinced a court that his tendency toward gambling with other people's money was a "handicap" and therefore protected under federal law.

Sykes describes a young man who stole a car from a parking lot and was killed while driving it, and his family responded by suing the proprietor of the parking lot for failing to take steps to prevent such thefts.

He relates the story of a man convicted of flashing others more than thirty times and who admitted to exposing himself more than ten thousand times. When he was turned down for a job as a park attendant due to his arrest record, he sued based on the argument that he had never exposed himself in a park—only in libraries and Laundromats. State employment officials agreed with him and ruled that he had probably been a victim of illegal job discrimination.[8]

If anything, the victim mentality in the United States has only gotten worse. Rather than taking responsibility for their lives, many people are trying to take the easy way out by establishing themselves as victims of society, the economy, a conspiracy, or some alleged discrimination. A victim mind-set causes people to focus on what they cannot do instead of what they can do. It is a recipe for continued failure.

> A victim mind-set causes people to focus on what they cannot do instead of what they can do. It is a recipe for continued failure.

When Ted Williams sobered up and started taking responsibility for his life, he recognized that his worst problem was entitlement. It was at the root of many of his difficulties, and it was, as he said, "a problem all my life. I expected the army to put me in communications, even though I didn't qualify. I expected radio stations to coddle me, even though I abused their trust."[9] It wasn't until he developed gratitude for what he did have and took responsibility that his life began to turn around.

2. We Have an Unrealistic Perspective of How Life Works

Life doesn't always work the way we'd like it to. If we had our way, it would be easier. It would be fair. It would be more fun. There'd be no pain and suffering. We would have to work only if we felt like it. And we would never die. But that isn't how life works. Life isn't easy. It's not fair. We do experience pain. Even the best of jobs includes unpleasant tasks and has times of drudgery. And every one of us will die.

Is that fair? No. Life isn't fair. Johnny Carson said, "If life were fair, Elvis would still be alive and all the impersonators would be dead." In life, we all get better than we deserve at times and worse than we deserve at others. And there is no guarantee that it will balance out in the end. The Bible says that God causes the sun to rise on the evil and the good

> "If life were fair, Elvis would still be alive and all the impersonators would be dead."
> —Johnny Carson

and he gives rain to the just and unjust.[10] We can get stuck asking why. But seeking answers to that question rarely helps. We may never know why things happen. If we focus on the why, we may never make real progress in our lives.

Another pitfall is comparing ourselves to others. That can lead to tremendous frustration and dissatisfaction, because you can always find someone better off than you are. I came across a humorous take on this recently written by a woman who says that in her next life, she would like to be a bear. She writes,

> If you're a bear, you get to hibernate. You do nothing but sleep for six months. I could deal with that. Before you hibernate, you're supposed to eat yourself stupid. I could deal with that, too. If you're a bear, you birth your children (who are the size of walnuts) while you're sleeping and wake to partially grown, cute cuddly cubs. I could definitely deal with that. If you're a mama bear, everyone knows you mean business. You swat anyone who bothers your cubs. If your cubs get out of line, you swat them too. I could deal with that. If you're a bear, your mate *expects* you to wake up growling. He *expects* that you will have hairy legs and excess body fat. Yup...Gonna be a bear![11]

> "Those things that hurt, instruct."
> —*Benjamin Franklin*

Benjamin Franklin wrote, "Those things that hurt, instruct." That's true, but only if you make an effort to understand how life works and accept it. Instead of focusing on *why* things happen, we are better off learning *how* things work. There are more lessons to be learned, and those lessons prepare us for future battles.

3. We Constantly Engage in "Blamestorming"

Another pattern that people fall into when they don't take responsibility is what I call "blamestorming." That's the creative process used for finding an appropriate scapegoat. One time I was counseling a man who had made a mess of his life and relationships. As we got started in the process of working on his issues, he told me, "There are three things wrong with me: my wife, my mother, and my son." Now that's blamestorming.

It's my understanding that insurance companies are the recipients of many creative excuses from drivers who refuse to take responsibility for themselves. I enjoy reading these kinds of things, and I hope you will, too. Here are some of my favorites:

> "As I reached the intersection, a hedge sprang up, obscuring my vision."
>
> "An invisible car came out of nowhere, struck my car, and vanished."
>
> "The telephone pole was approaching fast. I attempted to swerve out of its path when it struck my front end."
>
> "The indirect cause of this accident was a little guy in a small car with a big mouth."
>
> "I had been driving my car for four years when I fell asleep at the wheel and had an accident."
>
> "I was on my way to the doctor's with rear end trouble when my universal joint gave way, causing me to have an accident."
>
> "To avoid hitting the bumper of the car in front of me, I struck the pedestrian."

Author and editor Christopher Buckley tells a great story about an incident that occurred with actor David Niven, who starred in the original *Pink Panther* movie. Buckley writes,

My favorite faux pas story—we tell it with reverence in my family—happened to David Niven, who was a pal of my dad. He was the kindest man on earth, didn't have a mean bone in his body. A sweet, kind man. So he's at a white tie ball and he struck up a conversation with a man. They're standing at the foot of a grand staircase and two women appear at the top of the staircase and start to walk down and David nudges the man and says, "I say, that must be the ugliest woman I've ever seen in my life."

The man stiffens and says, "That's my wife."

Desperate for a lifeline, David says, "I mean the other one."

The man stiffens again and says, "That's my daughter!"

And David says, "I didn't say it!"

Buckley goes on to say, "We call that in our house the 'David Niven Defense.' It does come in handy."[12]

Any form of blamestorming may be handy in the moment, but it's not helpful in the long run. You can't grow and learn if your focus is on finding someone else to blame instead of looking at your own shortcomings.

4. We Give Away the Choice to Control Our Lives

Who is responsible for what happens in your life? Do you believe you should take personal responsibility? Or do you feel as if that is outside of your control and there's little or nothing you can do about it?

Psychologists say that some people possess an *internal* locus of control, where they rely primarily on themselves for the gains and losses in their lives. Others possess an *external* locus of control, where they blame others when something goes wrong. Which group is more successful? The group that takes personal responsibility. Which people are more content? The ones who take personal responsibility. Which people learn from their mistakes and keep growing and improving? The people who take responsibility.

Taking responsibility for your life is a choice. That doesn't mean you believe you are in control of everything in your life. That's not humanly possible. But you can take responsibility for yourself and every choice you have. I love the way chiropractor and author Eric Plasker looks at our choices in a piece called "I Choose My Life." You may be tempted to speed through the lines that follow, but please don't. There is insight to be gained in many of the choices Plasker puts together:

I choose to die.	I choose to live.
I choose to hate.	I choose to love.
I choose to close.	I choose to open.
I choose to cry.	I choose to laugh.
I choose to deny.	I choose to believe.
I choose to ignore.	I choose to hear.
I choose to be right.	I choose to relate.
I choose to scatter.	I choose to focus.
I choose to work.	I choose to play.
I choose to be angry.	I choose to accept.
I choose to despair.	I choose to hope.
I choose to give up.	I choose to persist.
I choose to suffer.	I choose to heal.
I choose to destroy.	I choose to create.
I choose to fail.	I choose to succeed.
I choose to extinguish.	I choose to ignite.
I choose to get by.	I choose to excel.
I choose to follow.	I choose to lead.
I choose to drift.	I choose to commit.
I choose my choices.	I choose my life.[13]

> "God asks no man whether he will accept life. That is not a choice. You must take it. The only choice is how."
>
> —*Henry Ward Beecher*

Abolitionist Henry Ward Beecher asserted, "God asks no man whether he will accept life. That is not a choice. You must take it. The only choice is how." How will you approach your life? Will you simply allow life to happen to you? Or will you seize the choices you make with enthusiasm and responsibility?

5. We Eliminate Any Possibility of Growth for Success

When we fail to take responsibility, not only do we develop a victim mentality, embrace an unrealistic perspective of how life works, engage in blamestorming, and give away the choice to control our lives, but we also eliminate any real possibility of growth for success. And that is the real tragedy of failing to be responsible.

Real success is a journey. We have to approach it with a long-term mind-set. We have to hang in there, stay focused, and keep moving forward. Excuses are like exits along the road of success that lead us nowhere. Taking the exit is easy, but it gets us off track. It is impossible to go from excuses to success. So we need to get back on the road, keep moving forward. If we want to do something and we take responsibility, we'll find a way. If not, we'll find an excuse. That may take the pressure off of us and make us feel better in the short term, but in the long run it won't make us successful.

Richard Bach said, "Argue for your limitations, and sure enough, they are yours." I may not like it, but I am responsible for who I am and where I am today. My present circumstances are a direct result of my past choices. My future will be the result of my current thoughts and actions. I am responsible, and so are you.

What Happens When We Learn to Be Responsible?

In *You Gotta Keep Dancin'*, Tim Hansel says, "Pain is inevitable but misery is optional." A similar thing can be said when it comes to taking responsibility. Losses are inevitable, but excuses are optional. When we move from excuses to responsibility, our lives begin to change dramatically. Here's how.

> **Losses are inevitable, but excuses are optional.**

1. We Take Our First Step in Learning

When you take responsibility for yourself, you take responsibility for your learning. The earlier you do this, the better the potential results. Professor and Pulitzer Prize–winning journalist William Raspberry had good advice regarding the importance of taking responsibility and making right choices when we are young. He observed,

> If you want to be thought of as a solid, reliable pillar of your community when you're fifty, you can't be an irresponsible, corner-cutting exploiter at twenty-five.... The time to worry about your reputation is before you *have* one. You determine your reputation by deciding who and what you are and by keeping that lofty vision of yourself in mind, even when you're having a rip-roaring good time.

If you take responsibility when you're young, you have a better chance of gaining wisdom as you get older. For some of us, it takes a long time. I sometimes feel that only after turning sixty-five did I begin to understand life. Now that I'm officially a senior citizen, I can say there are two things I know about my life. First, it has contained many surprises. My life didn't turn out like I thought it would. Some things turned out better than I imagined, some things worse. No matter who you are, it's impossible to know how your life will turn out.

Second, as long as I take responsibility for the things I can control in my life and try my best to learn from them, I can feel contented. Unfortunately, my personal challenge has been keeping myself from trying to control things outside my sphere of influence. Whenever I've overreached in that way and things have gone wrong, it has caused me to lose focus, waste energy, and feel discouraged. That has been a hard lesson for me.

If you can find the right balance where you take responsibility for the things you can control and let go of the things you cannot, you will accelerate your learning process. But even if you learn the lesson late, you can still benefit from it. That was true for Ted Williams. He was in his fifties when he finally took that first step. And as a result, he is learning and growing and improving his life.

2. We See Things in Their Proper Perspective

Taking responsibility for yourself does not mean taking yourself too seriously. When you do that, it carries over into a negative perspective in other areas of your life. Henri Frederic Amiel said, "We are never

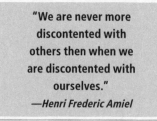

"We are never more discontented with others then when we are discontented with ourselves."
—Henri Frederic Amiel

more discontented with others than when we are discontented with ourselves." Taking responsibility doesn't mean cultivating a negative attitude. It means being willing to see things from a better perspective.

I've met people who allow their losses to overwhelm them. They say things like, "That incident ruined my life" or "That person makes me so mad." The truth is that nothing can ruin your life or make you mad without your permission! If you find yourself thinking along those lines, stop immediately. You have the power to choose another way of thinking, and you can learn how to do that by maintaining a proper perspective.

In 2009 when golfer Tom Watson was fifty-nine years old, he competed in the British Open on a very difficult course. He hadn't won a major tournament in twenty-five years, yet he was leading prior to the final hole of play. If he could par the final hole with a four, he would win. But his second shot took a hard bounce and went over the green. He ended up with a bogey, which led him into a playoff with Stewart Cink, who won the tournament.

What a disappointing loss. Media members were silent as they filed into the press tent after Watson's loss. What was the veteran golfer's response? "This ain't a funeral, you know," he joked. He was able to laugh about it, because he saw things in the proper perspective. It wasn't the end of the world for him.

The best learners are people who don't see their losses and failures as permanent. They see them as temporary. Or as Patricia Sellers once put it, "The most successful [people] at bouncing back view failure not like a cancer but, rather, like puberty: awkward and uncomfortable, but a transforming experience that precedes maturity."[14]

3. We Stop Repeating Our Failures

What's the major difference between people who succeed and people who don't? It's not failing. Both groups fail. However, the ones who take responsibility for themselves learn from their failures and *do not repeat them.*

If you think about it, how did you learn to walk when you were a baby? You tried something that didn't work and fell down. Then you tried something else that didn't work, and fell down. You probably tried *hundreds* of approaches—maybe thousands—all of which taught you what *didn't* work when it came to walking. And finally, you tried something that *did* work.

That's the way you learned to walk, eat, talk, ride a bike, throw a ball, and all the other basic tasks of living. Why would you think you'll ever get to a place where you can learn without failing and making mistakes? If you want to learn more, you need to do more. But you also need to pay attention to what's *not* working and make adjustments accordingly.

In his audiobook *The Psychology of Achievement*, Brian Tracy tells about four men who became millionaires by the age of thirty-five. He says each one was involved in an average of seventeen businesses before finding the right one for him. What's the message? To win, you can't just keep attempting the same thing over and over again. You must stop, take responsibility for your choices, reflect on what went wrong and what went right, make adjustments, and try again. That's the only way to be successful.

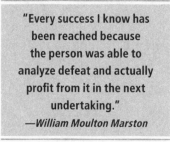

"Every success I know has been reached because the person was able to analyze defeat and actually profit from it in the next undertaking."
—*William Moulton Marston*

William Moulton Marston, the creator of Wonder Woman, remarked: "Every success I know has been reached because the person was able to analyze defeat and actually profit from it in the next undertaking." Failure isn't the best teacher. Neither is experience. Only evaluated experience teaches us. That's where the profit lies in any experience we have.

4. We Grow Stronger

Eleanor Roosevelt observed, "You gain strength, courage, and confidence by every experience in which you really stop to look fear in the face. You are able to say to yourself, 'I have lived through this horror. I can take the next thing that comes along.' You must do the thing you think you cannot do."

Every time that you take responsibility, face your fear, and move forward despite experiencing losses, failures, mistakes, and disappointments, you become stronger. And if you keep doing the things you ought to do when you ought to do them, the day will come when you will get to do the things you want to do when you want to do them.

This ability comes only if you take responsibility for becoming the person God created you to be, not someone else. In his book *Confidence: How To Succeed at Being Yourself*, Alan McGinnis wrote:

> The Hasidic rabbi, Zuscha, was asked on his deathbed what he thought the kingdom of God would be like. He replied, "I don't know. But one thing I do know. When I get there I am not going to be asked, 'Why weren't you Moses? Why weren't you David?' I am only going to be asked, 'Why weren't you Zuscha? Why weren't you fully you?' "[15]

We need to be asking ourselves a question similar to that one: Are we being ourselves? Are we taking full responsibility for that task? If our answer is yes, it makes us stronger day by day.

5. We Back Up Our Words With Our Behavior

The ultimate step in taking responsibility is making sure our actions line up with our words. Jeff O'Leary, author of *The Centurion Principles*, advised, "Sign your work at the end of each day. If you can't do that, find a new profession." If you are willing to put your name on

> "Sign your work at the end of each day. If you can't do that, find a new profession."
> —Jeff O'Leary

anything you do, that indicates a high level of integrity. To put your life on the line indicates an even higher one.

That's what author and consultant Frances Cole Jones describes in her book *The Wow Factor*. She writes,

In the Marines, "riggers"—the people who pack (i.e., reassemble after use) parachutes for other Marines—have to make at least one jump a month. Who packed their 'chute? They do: One of the parachutes that *they* packed for others to use is chosen at random, and the rigger has to "jump it." This system helps make sure that no one gets sloppy—after all, "The chute you're packing may be your own."

The Roman army used a similar technique to make sure bridges and aqueducts were safe: The person who designed the arches had to stand under each arch while the scaffolding was being removed.

If you want your company to last as long as Roman bridges have, ask yourself if everyone is *truly* responsible for outcomes by these measures—and if you yourself are. Are you performing every task with the concentration and commitment that you might if a life depended on it?[16]

It may sound like hyperbole when Jones asks if you are taking responsibility for the tasks you perform as if your life depends on it, but it's not really extreme. Why? Because our lives *do* depend on what we do. It took Ted Williams over fifty years and nearly cost him his life to learn that lesson. But the stakes are no less high for you and me. The life we have is the only life we get here on earth, and it's not a dress rehearsal. Every minute we waste is gone forever. We can either choose to take responsibility for what we do with it, or make excuses.

I hope, like me, you are choosing to face reality and take responsibility. If you do that, then you will be ready to dig in and focus on improvement, which is the subject of the next chapter.

5

Improvement: The Focus of Learning

How do you keep up with local happenings, national and international events, and the latest updates related to your career and areas of interest? Most people tap into social media, check their favorite blogs, and watch videos via the Internet. You can get pretty much any information you want at your fingertips using a smartphone, tablet, or computer.

Information before the Internet

Things were dramatically different when I was very young. Getting news and information took a bit of effort. Most people read the paper to keep up with what was happening in the world. Late-breaking news could be heard on the radio. And if you wanted to do research with any depth, you went to the library. But that began to change in the 1950s with the advent of television, and it blossomed in the 1960s with the establishment of the nightly network news broadcasts.

The undisputed champion of those broadcasts, the person who made them into regular staples in every home across America, was Walter Cronkite. From 1962 to 1981, Cronkite was anchor of the *CBS Evening News*. People called him "Uncle Walter" because he was so beloved and trusted. In fact, in 1972, two polls revealed that he was the "most trusted man in America."[1] He broke the news of the assassinations of John F. Kennedy, Martin Luther King Jr., and Bobby Kennedy. He covered Apollo 11's moon landing as well as the near-tragic Apollo 13 mission that had to be aborted. He covered Watergate, the Vietnam War, and the Iran hostage crisis. He delivered the news during two of the most eventful decades in modern American history. And many considered him to be the best ever. Brian Williams, the current *NBC Nightly News* anchor, said, "He was a founding father of our profession."[2]

Cronkite started out as a newspaper reporter and spent several years working for the United Press wire service. As a war correspondent covering World War II, he was fearless. He flew into enemy territory with airborne troops, rode along in a B-17 bomber on a bombing mission over Germany, and covered the Battle of the Bulge. Andy Rooney, who became a long-time contributor to *60 Minutes*, knew Cronkite in Europe during the war. In the 1990s, years after Cronkite retired, Rooney said, "Anyone who thinks of Walter Cronkite today as the authoritative father figure of television news would be surprised to know what a tough, competitive scrambler he was in the old Front Page tradition of newspaper reporting. He became the best anchorman there ever was in television because he knew news when he saw it and cared about it. He was relentlessly inquisitive. The subject of his interview always sensed that Cronkite was interested in what he had to say and knew a great deal about the issue himself."[3]

Cronkite was excellent, but he didn't start out that way. His career was successful because he was dedicated to continual improvement. He learned a key lesson early, when he was hired as a radio broadcaster for University of Oklahoma football games. Cronkite was a competent announcer, but he wasn't a football fanatic and he didn't know all the players. So he came up with a plan to help him identify players during the broadcast. "I devised an electric board by which spotters from the opposing teams would, by simply pressing a button, identify for me the names of those involved in each of the plays," Cronkite recalled.

Cronkite confidently set himself up for his first broadcast with the station's top executives and the sponsors in attendance. But from the first play, there were problems. "My spotters weren't worth a darn and the electric board was worthless," Cronkite remarked. He couldn't tell which players were which. He scrambled to find information in the program, and as the game went on, his play-by-play commentary fell behind so that the reaction of the crowd preceded his descriptions. In Cronkite's words, "The broadcast was a disaster." [4]

Remarkably the station's executives agreed to give him a second chance, but he knew that if he were to succeed, he would have to improve significantly. For that, Cronkite developed a new plan. He explains,

> I recruited as my spotter to punch the buttons on my electric machine, another station employee. He and I memorized the names and jersey numbers, ages, physical characteristics, and hometowns of every one of the thirty or forty members of every squad of every university we played—and, of course, the same for OU.
>
> We spent three or four hours a day drilling our memories. One of us would call out a single fact about each player—name or number. The other had to fill in all the details of his football biography.
>
> It was grueling, unglamorous work that began on Monday and went right up to game time the following Saturday. We

missed a lot of the partying that accompanied most football weekends. But the practice worked, and our broadcasts were highly successful from that second game on.

This experience early in my broadcast career taught me an invaluable lesson....For every story I expect to cover, I thoroughly research all the available material regarding the event, the background, and the major persons involved. And I don't design plans or labor-saving machinery that might permit me to skip this essential step in doing my job to the absolute limit of my ability. My motto: There are no shortcuts to perfection.[5]

How Do You Respond?

Most of us don't expect to achieve perfection. But we do want to perform at a higher level. That requires improvement. It's been said that the three most difficult words to say are, "I was wrong." When we make a mistake or fail, as Cronkite did on the early football broadcast, we don't want to admit it. Instead, we often do one of the following:

- **Blow Up:** We react with anger, resentment, blame, rationalization, and compensation.
- **Cover Up:** We try to hide our mistakes to protect our image and ourselves. A person who makes a mistake and then offers an excuse for it has made two mistakes.
- **Back Up:** We withdraw and begin distancing ourselves from those who might discover our mistake.
- **Give Up:** We throw up our hands and quit. We never address the mistake in a healthy way.

We react like the young Navy pilot who was engaged in maneuvers. The admiral had required absolute radio silence. However, the young pilot mistakenly turned on his radio and was heard to mutter, "Boy, am I fouled up!"

The admiral ordered all channels to be opened, and said, "Will the pilot who broke the radio silence identify himself immediately!"

A long silence ensued before the young pilot's voice was again heard over the airways: "I'm fouled up, but not that fouled up!"

Okay, so that's a silly joke, but people do act like that in real life. For example, John H. Holliday, who was the founder and editor of the *Indianapolis News*, stormed into the composing room one day, determined to find the culprit who had spelled *height* as *hight*. A check of the original copy indicated that he himself had been the one responsible for the misspelling. When he was told that he said, "Well, if that's the way I spelled it, that has to be right." For the next thirty years, the *Indianapolis News* misspelled the word *height*. That is the antithesis of Cronkite's reaction.

Insights on Improvement

The Stone Age didn't end because people ran out of stones. It ended because people kept learning and improving. The desire to improve themselves is in the DNA of all successful people. Getting better has been a personal passion with me for many years. Part of that involves striving to perform better day by day, but the desire for improvement has also prompted me to study others who share this passion. That has helped me to learn some important things when it comes to improvement, which I want to pass along to you.

1. Improving Yourself Is the First Step to Improving Everything Else

A few years ago I was leading a roundtable of twenty highly successful people. One man expressed his frustration at having plateaued in his business and personal life. He asked, "How can I keep from plateauing?" As we asked questions and he opened up, we made a discovery. He was more concerned about his personal success than he was his personal growth. That was getting in his way.

Success does not always bring growth, but personal growth will always add to our success. The highest reward for our toil is not what we get *for* it but what we become *by* it. The most important question is not, "What am I getting?" but "What am I becoming?"

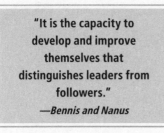

"It is the capacity to develop and improve themselves that distinguishes leaders from followers."
—Bennis and Nanus

Authors Warren Bennis and Burt Nanus asserted, "It is the capacity to develop and improve themselves that distinguishes leaders from followers." That same capacity is also what separates successful people from unsuccessful ones. And that ability is becoming more important every day.

The world is moving along at an incredible pace. I joked earlier about the end of the Stone Age. Some archaeologists believe that period lasted millions of years. The Bronze Age, which followed it, lasted roughly two thousand years. The Iron Age, which came next, was less than a thousand years. Each period in technological history has come faster and faster.

In the modern era knowledge, technology, and improvements continue to accelerate. Now that we live in the information age, the world is moving even faster. Economists at UC Berkeley recently calculated that in the year 2000, the total amount of information produced worldwide was the equivalent of 37,000 times as much information as the entire holdings in the Library of Congress. In 2003, the amount of new information created was more than double that.[6] And those numbers came from the time before Twitter, Facebook, YouTube, and other information-generating options were available.

The bottom line is clear. If you are not moving forward, the world is passing you by. If you want to improve your life, your family, your work, your economic situation, your influence, or anything else, you need to first improve yourself.

2. Improvement Requires Us to Move Out of Our Comfort Zone

Novelist Fyodor Dostoyevsky observed, "Taking a new step, uttering a new word, is what people fear most." Instead people should most fear the opposite—not taking the step. Why? Because if we don't step forward out of our comfort zone and into the unknown, we will not improve and grow. Security does not take us forward. It does not help us to overcome obstacles. It does not lead to progress. You'll never get anywhere interesting if you always do the safe thing. You must surrender security to improve.

What does it take to get us to move out of our comfort zone? In my observation, it requires two things:

Handling Our Aversion to Making Mistakes

Jack V. Matson, professor emeritus of environmental engineering at Pennsylvania State University and founding director of the Leonhard Center for the Enhancement of Engineering Education, develops courses in innovative design based on "intelligent fast failure." His philosophy is to stimulate creativity by encouraging students to risk failure and realize failure is essential to success.

When he was teaching at the University of Houston, he created a course called Failure 101 and organized an international conference, "Celebration of Failure."[7] In his Failure 101 course, Matson had his class build ice-cream-stick mock-ups of products no one would buy—from hamster hot tubs to kites to be flown in hurricanes. Matson says his students learned to equate failure with innovation instead of defeat, and it freed them up to get out of their comfort zone and try new things.

We can learn a lot from Matson. We need to fail quickly so that we can get it out of the way. If we're not failing or making mistakes, it means we're playing it too safe. Management expert Peter Drucker explained, "I would never promote a person into a high-level job who was not making mistakes. . . . Otherwise he is sure to be mediocre."

Mistakes are not failures. They are proof that we are making an effort. When we understand that, we can more easily move out of our comfort zone, try something new, and improve.

Overcoming a Life Controlled by Feelings

Legendary Baltimore Oriole shortstop Cal Ripken Jr. played in more consecutive baseball games than any other player: 2,632 games. That means he didn't miss a single game in more than sixteen seasons! When asked if he ever went to the ballpark with aches and pains, Ripken replied, "Yeah, just about every day."

Ripken didn't allow his feelings—even feelings of physical pain—to overwhelm him or keep him from performing. He pushed through them. If we want to succeed in getting out of our comfort zone so that we can improve, we need to follow his example.

Improvement demands a commitment to grow long after the mood in which it was made has passed. Speaker Peter Lowe once told me,

"The most common trait I have found in successful people is that they conquered the temptation to give up." Not being controlled by our feelings means that we can face our fears, get out of our comfort zone, and try new things. That is an important part of innovation.

> "The most common trait I have found in successful people is that they conquered the temptation to give up."
> —Peter Lowe

3. Improvement Is Not Satisfied with "Quick Fixes"

We live in a society with destination disease. Too many people want to do enough to "arrive," and then they want to retire. My friend Kevin Myers says it this way: "Everyone is looking for a quick fix, but what they really need is fitness. People who look for fixes stop doing what's right when pressure is relieved. People who pursue fitness do what they should no matter what." That's true. Losers don't lose because they focus on losing. They lose because they focus on just getting by.

> Losers don't lose because they focus on losing. They lose because they focus on just getting by.

Improvement doesn't come to people who fixate on quick fixes. It comes to the slow but steady people who keep working at getting better. If you have a quick fix mindset, then you need to shift it to continuous improvement. That means doing two things:

Accept the Fact that Improvement Is a Never-Ending Battle

I believe all of us can identify with the poet Carl Sandberg, who said, "There is an eagle in me that wants to soar and a hippopotamus in me that wants to wallow in the mud." The key to success is following the impulse to soar more than the desire to wallow. And that is a never-ending struggle—at least it has been for me. I believe any successful person would be honest in saying, "I got to the top the hard way—fighting my own laziness and ignorance every step of the way."

Author and leadership expert Fred Smith, who mentored me for many years, said that something in human nature tends to make us want to find a plateau and stay there where it's comfortable. What he was describing was the temptation to disengage from the battle for improvement. Fred said, "Of course, all of us need to plateau for a time. We climb and then plateau for assimilation. But once we've assimilated what we've learned, we climb again. It's unfortunate when we've done our last climb. When we have made our last climb, we are old, whether forty or eighty."

If you are just beginning your improvement journey, don't be discouraged. Your starting point doesn't matter. Everyone who has gotten to where he is, started where he was. What matters is where you end up. And you get there by continuing to fight the improvement battle. As you do, make this your motto:

I'm not where I'm supposed to be,
I'm not what I want to be,
But I'm not what I used to be.
I haven't learned how to arrive;
I've just learned how to keep on going.

If you can live those words, you will eventually be successful.

Accept the Fact That Improvement Is a Result of Small Steps

People today are looking for a secret to success. They want a magic bullet, an easy answer, a single thing that will catapult them to fortune or fame. Success generally doesn't work that way. As Andrew

Wood observed, "Success in most things comes not from some gigantic stroke of fate, but from simple, incremental progress." That's pretty boring, isn't it? It may not be exciting, but it is true. Small differences over time create a big difference! Improvement is achieved in inches, not giant leaps.

> Small differences over time create a big difference! Improvement is achieved in inches, not giant leaps.

In my early years, I would see and hear a successful person and say to myself, "I will never be able to achieve that." And I would become discouraged. Why? Because I saw the giant gap between that person and me. The difference between where I was and where that person was appeared to be insurmountable. But what I didn't realize back then was that the progress these people had made and the gains they had won had come through small steps—small victories of will, little denials of self, faithfulness in very little things. Most people were unaware of their hidden steps. Like me, they saw only their accumulation in the results.

Writer and artist Elbert Hubbard observed, "The line between failure and success is so fine that we scarcely know when we pass it—so fine that we are often on the line and we do not know it. How many a man has thrown up his hands at a time when a little more effort, a little more patience, would have achieved success?" That's why we need to dedicate ourselves to small steps of improvement. Who knows if the next small step will provide the breakthrough we've been seeking?

4. Improvement Is a Daily Commitment

David D. Glass, the president and chief executive officer of Walmart, was once asked why he admired Sam Walton, the founder of the organization. His answer was, "There's never been a day in his life, since I've known him, that he didn't improve in some way." What an accomplishment! That shows a great commitment to continuous improvement.

Fairly early in my development on the personal growth journey, I heard something from Earl Nightingale that changed my life. He said, "If you study a subject every day for one hour a day, five days a week, in five years you will become an expert in that area." That was when I made the commitment to improve in the area of leadership a daily one.

Some things simply have to be done every day. You know the old saying, "An apple a day keeps the doctor away"? Well, eating seven apples all at once isn't going to give you the same benefit. If you want to improve, intentional growth needs to be a habit. A habit is something I do continually, not once in a while. Motivation may get you going, but the positive habits you develop and practice consistently are what keep you improving.

As I have worked to improve on a day-by-day basis, two words have helped me to stay on track. The first is *intention*. Every morning as I start my day, I intend to learn something that day. This develops a mind-set in me to look for things that will help me improve.

The other word is *contemplation*. Time alone is an essential for self-improvement. When I spend time thinking about my challenges, experiences, and observations, it allows me to gain perspective. I can evaluate any losses and I can learn from them. Contemplation time by myself also gives me time to do positive self-talk. Motivational humorist Al Walker stated, "The most important words we will ever utter are those words we say to ourselves, about ourselves, when we are by ourselves." During these "conversations" we can beat ourselves up and make ourselves

> "The most important words we will ever utter are those words we say to ourselves, about ourselves, when we are by ourselves."
> —*Al Walker*

feel really small, or we can learn and build ourselves up so that we become better.

If you want to spend some time each day to try to improve yourself, you might want to begin by asking yourself three questions at the end of the day, as I do. They are:

- What did I learn today? What spoke both to my heart and my head?
- How did I grow today? What touched my heart and affected my actions?
- What will I do differently? Unless I can state specifically what I plan to do differently, I won't learn anything.

One of the things I *don't* do is compare myself to others during that time. There's a reason for that. My desire is to not become superior to anybody else. I only want to be superior to my former self. Intention and contemplation assist me in doing that.

Make Improvement Intentional

Improvement is within the reach of anyone, no matter how experienced or green, educated or ignorant, rich or poor. To start improving today, do these three things:

1. Decide You Are Worth Improving

To improve yourself, you must believe you can improve. Author Denis Whitley has a wonderful definition for personal development. He says that it is the conviction that there is value in your dreams. "Personal

> "Personal development is the belief that you are worth the effort, time, and energy needed to develop yourself. It gives you permission to invest in yourself so you can develop your own potential."
> —*Denis Whitley*

development," he says, "is the belief that you are worth the effort, time, and energy needed to develop yourself. It gives you permission to invest in yourself so you can develop your own potential."

You can invest in yourself. You don't need anyone's dreams but your own. And you don't need to become anyone other than yourself at your best. The great philosopher Thomas Carlyle once wrote, "Let each become all that he was created capable of being." I can't think of a better definition of success. Life challenges us every day to develop our capabilities to the fullest. We're successful when we reach for the highest that's within us—when we give the best we have. Life doesn't require us to always come out on top. It asks only that we do our best to improve at whatever level of experience we are currently on.

2. Pick an Area to Improve

There is a funny story about a wealthy Texan who died. When his attorney asked the entire family to gather for the reading of the will, relatives came from near and far to see if they were included in the bequests.

On the day they were assembled, the lawyer somberly opened the will and began to read:

"To my cousin Ed, I leave my ranch."

"To my brother Jim, I leave my money market accounts."

"To my neighbor and good friend, Fred, I leave my stocks."

"And finally, to my cousin George, who always sat around and never did anything, but wanted to be remembered in my will, I want to say, 'Hi, George.' "

Most of us either want to improve nothing, like George, or we are so impatient to become all that we can that we try to improve all that we are at the same time. Those are both mistakes. We need to focus. Noted psychologist William Jones advised, "If you would be rich, you will be rich; if you would be good, you will be good; if you would be learned, you will be learned. But wish for one thing exclusively, and don't at the same time wish for a hundred other incompatible things just as strongly."

You will have plenty of time to improve other areas of your life. Focus on the one now that makes the most of your strengths and is closest to your sense of purpose. Take the advice of Earl Nightingale who suggested spending an hour a day improving in that area. Then take it slow but steady. We always overestimate what we can get done in a day or a week. But we underestimate what we can get done in a year. Just imagine what you will be able to get done in five years.

3. Find Opportunities to Improve in the Wake of Your Losses

Focused, strategic improvement is important to success. But so is learning from our losses as they come. I will address that more specifically in the chapters on adversity, problems, and bad experiences. However, let me say this. Some lessons in life cannot wait. You must make the most of them when they occur. If you don't examine what went wrong while the details are fresh, you may lose the ability to learn the lesson. Besides, if you neglect to learn the lesson immediately, you may experience the loss again!

Business professor George Knox said, "When you cease to be

better, you cease to be good. When you stop growing, you cease to be useful—a weed in the garden of prosperity.... We are what we are today because we were what we were yesterday. And our thoughts today determine our actions tomorrow." Those who learn from their losses give themselves that permission. As your friend, I give it to you also. Knowledge may come from study, but wisdom comes from learning and improving in the wake of your mistakes.

> Knowledge may come from study, but wisdom comes from learning and improving in the wake of your mistakes.

I always try to remember that I am a work in progress. When I maintain that perspective, I realize that I don't have to be perfect. I don't have to have it all together. I don't need to try to have all the answers. And I don't need to learn everything in a day. When I make a mistake, it's not because I'm a failure or worthless. I just didn't do something right because I still haven't improved enough in some part of the process. And that motivates me to keep growing and improving. If I don't know something, it's an opportunity to try to improve in a new area.

I'm in it for the long haul. I try to be like industrialist Ian MacGregor, who said, "I work on the same principle as people who train horses. You start with low fences, easily achieved goals, and work up." When I got started, my fences were embarrassingly low. But in time I was able to raise them. Today, I'm still raising them little by little. That's the only way I know how to keep improving, and I always want to keep doing that, because improvement is the focus of learning.

> "I work on the same principle as people who train horses. You start with low fences, easily achieved goals, and work up."
> —Ian MacGregor

6

Hope: The Motivation of Learning

Not long ago I was signing books after speaking to a large crowd at a convention center. Whenever I speak, I try to make myself available to sign books, shake hands, and chat with people. This particular day the line was long, and I was signing as quickly as I could to try to get to everyone waiting.

A lady stepped up and handed me a book to sign, and she said, "For the last eight years I have been reading your books and listening to your teaching. You have given to me a wonderful gift, and I am grateful."

I stopped writing and for a moment I wondered what that gift might be. Was it the simplicity of my teaching? Practicality? Humor? I was curious, so I asked, "What is the wonderful gift I have given you?"

"Hope." She continued, "Whenever I read your books or listen to you, I leave with hope. Thank you."

She took her book and left, but her words did not leave me. I was very grateful, because my desire is always to add value to people, and if she became more hopeful, then I felt I had indeed added value to her.

As you may know, leadership is one of my passions. I learn about it every day, and it is one of my great joys to teach it to others. Former cabinet member John W. Gardner said, "The first and last task of a leader is to keep hope alive—the hope that we can finally find our way through to a better world—despite the day's action, despite our own inertness, shallowness, and wavering resolve." The great general Napoleon said even more simply: "Leaders are dealers in hope."

As a leader and writer, I want to be someone who gives others hope. I believe that if a leader helps people believe the impossible is possible, it makes the impossible probable. So as you read this chapter, regardless of what losses you face or difficulties you must overcome, keep your head up. Losses in life are never fun, but there is one loss no one can afford to experience—the loss of hope. If you lose hope, that may be your last loss, because when hope is gone, so is motivation and the ability to learn.

> **Losses in life are never fun, but there is one loss no one can afford to experience— the loss of hope.**

Hope Is a Beautiful Thing

In 1979 I wrote my first book, *Think on These Things*. It grew out of my desire to help people think upon the things that would build up their lives. One chapter was on the subject of hope. In it, I wrote the following words:

What does hope do for mankind?
- Hope shines brightest when the hour is darkest.
- Hope motivates when discouragement comes.
- Hope energizes when the body is tired.
- Hope sweetens when the bitterness bites.

- Hope sings when all melodies are gone.
- Hope believes when the evidence is limited.
- Hope listens for answers when no one is talking.
- Hope climbs over obstacles when no one is helping.
- Hope endures hardship when no one is caring.
- Hope smiles confidently when no one is laughing.
- Hope reaches for answers when no one is asking.
- Hope presses toward victory when no one is encouraging.
- Hope dares to give when no one is sharing.
- Hope brings the victory when no one is winning.

In short, hope gives. It gives to us even when we have little or nothing left. It is one of the most precious things we have in life.

Hope is inspiring. It gives us the motivation for living and learning. I say that for several reasons:

1. Hope Says Yes to Life

Author and theologian Paul Tillich was asked about the central theme of his book *The Courage to Be* shortly before he died. Tillich said the book was about real courage: saying yes to life in spite of all the hardship and pain which are part of human existence. It takes courage to find something positive and meaningful about ourselves and life every day. That, he said, was the key to living life more fully. "Loving life," he stated, "is perhaps the highest form of the courage to be."

Where does a person find the courage to say yes to life? I believe it comes from hope. In life, you must expect trouble. You must expect adversity. You must expect conflict. But those facts don't mean you have to lose hope. You can take the advice of Ann Landers, who said, "Expect trouble as an inevitable part of life and when it comes, hold your head high, look it squarely in the eye, and say, 'I will be bigger than you. You cannot defeat me.' "

I believe that is what President Barack Obama did as he made his run for the White House in 2008. It was an important day in America's history on January 20, 2009, when the first African-American became president of the United States. Regardless of your political leanings, that election answered a lot of questions about the color of people's skin and their potential. That morning I picked up a newspaper and read the following full-page ad:

> You can't abolish slavery.
> You can't build a railroad from the Atlantic to the Pacific.
> You can't give women the right to vote.
> You can't fly an airplane from New York to Paris.
> You can't defeat Nazi Germany.
> You can't devise a plan to rebuild war-ravaged Europe.
> You can't cure polio.
> You can't allow black children and white children to go to school
>   together.
> You can't put a man on the moon.
> You can't pass a Civil Rights act.
> You can't beat the Russians in hockey.
> You can't help bring down the Berlin Wall.
> You can't map the human genome.
> You can't elect a black man president of the United States.
> What next, America? Because whatever it is, the answer is yes, we can.[1]

That day in America, hope was a beautiful thing. The word *yes* was on the lips of the people. That's what hope does. Embrace it and it will empower you.

2. Hope Fills Us with Energy

It's been said that a person can live forty days without food, four days without water, four minutes without air, but only four seconds without hope. Why? Hope provides the power that energizes us with life. Hope is a powerful thing. It keeps us going when times are tough. It creates excitement in us for the future. It gives us reasons to live. It gives us strength and courage.

I think it's no coincidence that people who suffer with depression often lack energy. Lack of hope and lack of energy usually go hand in hand. People who have a hard time believing in themselves have a difficult time finding the energy to cope with life and its challenges. In contrast, hope-filled people are energetic. They welcome life and all that it brings—even its challenges.

3. Hope Focuses Forward

My dad loves to tell stories and jokes. One of his favorites goes like this:

"You look downhearted, old man. What are you worried about?" asked Joe.

"My future," Bill replied.

"What makes your future look so hopeless?" was the question.

"My past," was the answer.

Okay, now you know where I got my love for this kind of humor!

I can certainly identify with Bill. Perhaps you can, too. Our yesterdays have a tendency to invade our todays with negativism, stealing our joy and hope. If we dwell on them too much, they threaten to rob us of our future. That's why I like these words of Ralph Waldo Emerson: "Finish each day and be done with it.... You have done what you could; some blunders and absurdities no doubt crept in; forget them as soon as you can. Tomorrow is a new day; you shall begin it well and serenely."

Hope always has a future. It leans forward with expectation. It desires to plan for tomorrow. And that opens us up to greater possibilities. There's a story of a salesman from the eastern United States who arrived at a frontier town somewhere in the Old West. As the salesman was talking with the owner of the general store, a rancher came in. The owner excused himself to take care of the customer.

The rancher gave the storekeeper a list of things he needed, but he wanted credit to purchase them.

"Are you doing any fencing this spring?" asked the storekeeper.

"Sure am, Will," said the rancher.

"Fencing in or fencing out?"

"Fencing in. Taking in another 360 acres across the creek."

"Good to hear it, Josh. You got the credit. Just tell Harry out back what you need."

The salesman was confused. "I've seen all kinds of credit systems," he said, "but never one like that. How does it work?"

"Well," said the storekeeper, "if a man's fencing out, that means he's on the defensive, just trying to keep what he's got. But if he's fencing in, he's growing and getting bigger. I always give credit to a man who's fencing in, because that means he's got hope."

Are you looking forward? Do you have hope for the future? If you have high expectations for tomorrow, then you probably want to meet it at your best. How do you do that? By growing, learning, and improving. Lack of hope breeds indifference toward the future. Hope brings motivation.

4. Hope Is a Difference Maker

Recently I read *No Ordinary Times*, a biography of Franklin and Eleanor Roosevelt during World War II, written by Doris Kearns Goodwin. Many pages of the book were dedicated to England and Prime Minister Winston Churchill's leadership during the dark days of conflict with the Nazis.

Churchill certainly was a leader of hope to his people. As the Nazis swept across Europe and then mercilessly bombed England during the Blitz, the task of defeating Hitler and the Nazis seemed impossible. Yet, despite the odds against them, the British prevailed.

How was one relatively small nation, standing alone for quite a long time, able to withstand the Nazi onslaught? When Winston Churchill was asked what was England's greatest weapon versus the Nazis, he responded with one word: *hope.*

Hope is our greatest asset and the greatest weapon we can use to battle our losses when they seem to be mounting. It is powerful, and that is why I call it a difference maker. What does hope do for us?

- Hope looks for the lesson in defeat instead of just leaving you feeling defeated.
- Hope discovers what *can* be done instead of what *can't* be done.
- Hope regards problems, small or little, as opportunities.
- Hope lights a candle instead of cursing the darkness.
- Hope opens doors where despair closes them.
- Hope draws its strength from *what can be* instead of *what was.*
- Hope cherishes no illusions nor does it yield to cynicism.
- With hope, failure is a skipping stone. Without hope, failure is a tombstone.

If you want to find the motivation to learn in the face of your losses, to keep working to get better tomorrow than you are today, to reach your potential and fulfill your purpose, then make use of the difference maker. Embrace hope.

How to Cultivate Hope

Since hope is such a beautiful thing, this question has to be asked: "Can anyone have it?" The answer is yes! Regardless of your present situation, background, personality, upbringing, or circumstances, you can be a person of hope. Doing the following three things will help you to get there.

1. Realize That Hope Is a Choice

British clergyman G. Campbell Morgan told the story of a man whose shop had been burned in the great Chicago fire of 1871. The man arrived at the ruins the next morning carrying a table. He set up the table in the midst of the charred debris, and above it placed a sign that said, "Everything lost except wife, children, and hope. Business will be resumed as usual tomorrow morning."[2]

That man's response is one that I truly admire. After such a heavy loss, where did he get his hope? From his circumstances? Certainly not. From good timing? No. From other victims of the fire? There's no indication that he did. How many others faced the future with such positive determination? If this man saw a bright future for himself and his family, it was because he made a choice to have hope.

Hope is in the DNA of men and women who learn from their losses. When times are tough, they choose hope, knowing that it will motivate them to learn and turn them from victims into victors.

Some people say choosing hope is a pie-in-the-sky approach to life. It's unrealistic, they claim. I disagree. In *The Dignity of Difference*, Jonathan Sacks writes, "One of the most important distinctions I have learned in the course of reflection on Jewish history is the difference between *optimism* and *hope*. Optimism is the belief that things will get better. Hope is the faith that, together, we can make things better. Optimism is a passive virtue, hope an active one. It takes no courage to be an optimist, but it takes a great deal of courage to have hope."[3]

I believe everyone is capable of choosing hope. Does it take courage? Yes. Because hope can be disappointing. But I am convinced that the courage of choosing hope is always rewarded.

2. Change Your Thinking

In general we get what we expect in life. I don't know why that is true, but it is. Norman Cousins remarked, "The main trouble with despair is that it is self-fulfilling. People who fear the worst tend to invite it. Heads that are down can't scan the horizon for new openings. Bursts of energy do not spring from a spirit of defeat. Ultimately, helplessness leads to hopelessness." If your expectations for life are negative, you end up experiencing a lot of negatives. And those negatives are compounded and become especially painful, because negative expectations cause a person not to learn from their losses. We become like the negative man who said, "If I could drop dead right now, I'd be the happiest man on earth!"

> "The main trouble with despair is that it is self-fulfilling."
> —*Norman Cousins*

That makes light of it, but negative thinking is really no laughing matter. The good news is that you don't have to live with it. You can change your thinking from a negative mind-set, in which you feel hopeless, don't learn from your losses, and are tempted to give up, to a positive mind-set, in which you believe things can get better, you learn from your mistakes, and you never quit.

Recently I met Bob Wosczyk during a break at one of my conferences. He gave me a copy of his book *Who Says the Fat Lady Has to Sing?* The reference to a fat lady comes from the opera because the finale of an opera is traditionally sung by the soprano, who was often heavyset. When she sings her incredible final solo, you know the opera is finished. But nowadays the phrase is used in reference to anything. People say "It's not over until the fat lady sings" to mean there's still time for the outcome to change. Bob takes exception to the idea that we ever give up, especially on our dreams. He writes:

We have all heard the expression, "It's not over until the fat lady sings." The implication here is that when the fat lady sings, the game is over and the will to continue fighting is lost. We choose to stay down on the canvas of life, afraid to get up and go another round because we are too beaten down to absorb any more punishment. We would rather quit on our dreams than continue to fight in pain, never knowing what could have been.

When we finally allow the fat lady to sing, we are forever haunted by the ghost of "What if?" "What if I quit too soon?" "What if I was on the right path, but then gave up too early?" "What if my very next action could have been the one that finally turned it all around?" "What if I could have lived the life I really wanted, rather than the life I had to settle for?"

The question I pose in this book is this: Why does it ever have to be over...? When did it become okay to give up, lay down, roll over, and attempt to sleep away our problems, losing our energy and enthusiasm for life? Who made quitting an option? Who says the fat lady has to sing?

What we don't understand is that most people quit when they are just inches away from their goal. They never realize just how close they actually are to reaching their dream.[4]

> "Who made quitting an option?"
> —*Bob Wosczyk*

Why do people give up as Bob describes? Because they lose hope. Their thinking is negative, their expectations are low, and they don't know how to get out of that pattern. The answer may not be easy, but it is simple. They need to change the way they think about themselves and the losses they experience. In life, we see what we are prepared to see. That is a result of our thinking. What we see is what we get. And that determines the outcome in much of what we do.

My favorite baseball hitter of all time was Tony Gwynn, who played for the Padres when I lived in San Diego. Year after year he led the league in batting average. One time I attended a game with a friend of Tony's. As we sat watching the game, Tony came up to bat and I said to Tony's friend, "I love to watch him hit. Why do you think he's so successful?"

"He expects to get a hit every time he bats," the friend replied.

Did Tony *always* get a hit? Of course not. That's impossible. The greatest hitters of all time fail six times out of ten. But those misses did not determine his expectation. He always believed in himself and his ability to get a hit. We should imitate him, because too often our main limitation comes from our expectations.

In his book *The Making of the Achiever*, Allan Cox wrote,

The achiever looks around the corner in anticipation of additional good things that await him. All he has to do, he believes, is show a little determination to get there. He rejects the notion of "can't." As a result, he is able to open more doors than others, strike better deals and attract more energetic and resourceful people to work with him. He sets higher standards and gets others to help him meet them. He wins confidence and nurtures vitality in others. He expects to succeed. When combined with desire, expectancy produces hope. And hope makes all things possible. Living the expectant life is simply an act of good judgment.

As I said, it's simple, but it's not easy. If you have been a negative thinker whose motivation has been rarely fueled by hope, then you must make a determination every day to try to renew your hope, change your thinking for the better, and believe that good things can and will happen to you. Doing these things can literally change your life.

3. Win Some Small Victories

If you are able to tap into your hope and become more positive in your thinking, that's a great start. But it's not enough. Positive thinking must be followed by positive doing. If you want to succeed big, then start by trying for a small victory. Nothing encourages hope like success.

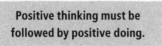

> Positive thinking must be followed by positive doing.

If you are able to win small victories, it encourages you. It raises your morale. When you experience a win once, you begin to understand how it works. You get better at succeeding, and after winning several victories you begin to sense that bigger victories are nearly within your grasp.

Creating a positive environment with positive experiences can go a long way to encourage you to keep hoping, keep trying, and keep learning. Take a look at the difference between what happens when people sense victory and when they sense defeat:

WHEN PEOPLE SENSE VICTORY	WHEN PEOPLE SENSE DEFEAT
They sacrifice to succeed.	They give as little as possible.
They look for ways to win.	They look for excuses.
They become energized.	They become tired.
They follow the game plan.	They forsake the game plan.
They help other team members.	They hurt others.

Winning small victories can change your entire outlook on life. Neil Clark Warren, the founder of eHarmony, spent his earlier career counseling married couples. During that time he realized that his primary goal in counseling should be to help couples, even deeply troubled ones, to improve even a small amount. When couples see even a small improvement—as little as 10 percent—they gain hope. And hope is a powerful motivation for change and learning.

The Power of Hope

One of the most hopeful times in people's lives is when they are looking forward to the birth of a child. The world of possibilities for that child seems nearly limitless, especially for a child born in a free country, like the United States, that offers so many opportunities. The parents of Jim Abbott were hopeful, even though they were little more than kids themselves when Jim was born. But their optimism for Jim was also shaken when they discovered that their brand-new baby boy was born without a right hand.

Jim's parents, Mike and Kathy, sought answers for the birth defect.

So did their doctors. But they never found a specific reason for it. It was something that had merely happened, and the teenage parents had to find a way to deal with it.

Jim played like a normal kid, and he didn't seem to be slowed down too much by the absence of a hand, but when he got to be five, the experts advised Mike and Kathy to send him to the Mary Free Bed Rehabilitation Hospital in Grand Rapids, more than one hundred miles away from their home in Flint, Michigan, so that he could be fitted with a prosthesis and be trained to use it. Back in those days, that meant a hook.

Jim's parents followed the advice, and Jim did receive a hook and learn to use it. He worked at it alongside kids with severe disabilities, such as a child who was learning to brush her teeth with her feet—because she had no arms. But there came a moment in the hospital when they realized that Jim didn't really belong there. Their best hope would be to treat him as a normal kid. Jim's parents removed him from the hospital and took him home.

During the drive home, Mike told Kathy, "We don't have a problem. We've got a blip on the screen. We can handle this. We could make it a problem if we want it to be a problem. But, it's no problem anymore."[5] Jim later wrote, "On that two-hour trip to Flint [going home from the children's hospital], we'd get our strength back. Mom and Dad felt hope, even optimism, for the first time beginning to focus not on what I lacked but what I had."[6]

Two of the things Jim had were a love for sports and good athletic ability. When Jim was six, his father bought him a baseball glove. He loved it. He spent hours throwing a rubber baseball at a brick wall, bettering his aim and arm strength, and figuring out how to get his glove from his right arm onto his left hand so that he could field the ball when it bounced back. Once he came up with a system, he kept improving his speed and fluidity. As he got better, he stood closer to the wall so that he had to make the transition more quickly to catch the ball.

Baseball wasn't Jim's only love. He played every sport. He'd go out with the neighborhood boys and be part of every pickup game. At first, nobody would pick him. There were times when he came home discouraged and wanted to give up. But his dad wouldn't allow it. Mike would send his son back out to the playground to keep trying. He had hope for Jim and wanted him to learn to persevere and overcome obstacles. He was preparing Jim for the road ahead.

Jim says, "The thing about a disability is, it's forever."[7] It's not going away, so you have to learn how to deal with it. How did Jim do that? He played every sport and did everything he could to improve himself. And he started to get some recognition because he was good—so good, in fact, that he dreamed of someday playing baseball at the highest level, an aspiration he shared for the first time publicly when he was twelve. "It seemed like a lot to hope for, but I had plenty of hope, and plenty of help," Jim explains.[8]

Hope Pays Off

"I was no prodigy. I was cut from the freshman basketball team at Flint Central High School. I made the freshman baseball team, but didn't get a hit the whole season. It was a long time before I separated myself from boys my age on athletic fields," says Jim.[9] But separate himself he did. As a high school sophomore, he played varsity baseball. When he was a junior, the coach told him he was the ace. Jim batted .367 that year and helped his team become city champions.

That year his coach also recruited him to play football as the backup quarterback. He was reluctant, but his coach insisted. Jim ended up starting in the playoffs and nearly took the team to a state championship.

As a senior, Jim played first base, pitched (winning ten games with an ERA of 0.76), and batted cleanup (.427 average). His team won the conference championship, and the Toronto Blue Jays drafted him. But Jim had his heart set on playing for the University of Michigan, which he did for three years. He was an All-American, winning two Big Ten championships. And he played on the Olympic baseball team. He pitched the gold-medal game in the 1988 Summer Olympics in Seoul, South Korea.

Jim's dream came true when he was again drafted, this time by the California Angels. He was the eighth pick of the 1988 draft. He expected to spend a long time in the minors, working his way up. But much to his surprise, he made the major league roster on opening day of his first year as a member of the starting rotation of pitchers.

Hope Pays Back

Jim played major league baseball for ten years. Some seasons he was fantastic. Other years he struggled. A particular highlight of his professional career was the no-hitter he pitched in 1993 at Yankee Stadium. There were many things about playing major league baseball that he misjudged or didn't expect. But the thing that turned out surprising him the most was the attention he got from children with disabilities similar to his.

Jim remembered what a thrill it was for him to meet a major league ballplayer, so the fact that kids would want to talk to him or get his autograph wasn't a surprise. But he didn't expect parents and their physically challenged kids to seek him out as they did. Jim wrote,

I didn't see them coming, not in the numbers they did. I didn't expect the stories they told, or the distance they traveled to tell them, or the desperation revealed in them.

They were shy and beautiful, and they were loud and funny, and they were, like me, somehow imperfectly built. And, like me, they had parents nearby, parents who willed themselves to believe that this accident of circumstances or nature was not a life sentence, and that the spirits inside these tiny bodies were greater than the sums of their hands and feet.[10]

Jim read and answered every letter sent to him by one of these children or their parents. He would stop whatever he was doing in the clubhouse whenever Tim Mead, then the PR manager for the Angels (and now the club's vice president of communications), would poke his head in and say, "Hey Jim, got a minute?" Jim would go out to meet children and spend a few minutes talking with them. He'd find out what position they played, ask how they batted, ask them to show him how they worked their glove. And Jim would talk to the parents:

I would tell them about my parents. They'd made me feel special for what I was, and yet treated me like I was every other kid from the neighborhood. I would tell them about my frustrations, and their words, "This is something to be lived up to." I asked them to see that that, and so much else, were possible, and amazing things could happen. My parents had done that for me, and they could do the same for their boy."[11]

Jim says he never turned down a single child, even when he was exhausted or discouraged or busy. Why? He wanted to give them hope! He wanted them to understand that so much was possible for them. Jim says, "I knew these kids and I knew how far a little boy or girl could run with fifty words of reassurance."[12]

Jim retired from baseball in 1999. In his career he pitched 1,674 innings, struck out 888 batters, and won 87 games.[13] He had lived out a dream, one that few people would have thought possible. He gave himself to baseball, and baseball gave him a lot in return. Jim sums up, "Maybe the greatest gift [from baseball] was that it helped me come to peace with the burden of being different." But he also points out, "The lesson had to be learned through losing, painful as it was."[14]

How was Jim Abbott able to learn from his losses? Because he had hope. He kept believing, and he kept trying. Hope provided the motivation for learning. And he used that motivation to learn more and go farther than others believed was possible. That is the power of hope.

7

Teachability: The Pathway of Learning

A husband and wife were out golfing together. On the par-four eighth hole, the husband hooked his drive into the woods. Angrily he prepared to expend a shot by pitching back out onto the fairway.

"Wait, dear," his wife said. "See the barn over there between you and the green? If I open the doors on both sides, you could hit it right through the barn onto the green."

She opened the doors, and the husband hit a screaming three iron, which ricocheted off the barn wall and hit his wife right between the eyes, killing her instantly.

A year later, the same fellow was golfing the same course with a friend. At the eighth hole, he hooked his drive again. He was all set to pitch out into the fairway, when his friend stopped him.

"Wait a minute. The only thing blocking your shot to the green is that barn. If I open up both doors, you can probably shoot right through the barn to the green."

"No way!" screamed the man. "Not again. I tried that last year and got a seven!"

Okay, I admit that's an awful joke. But as a golfer, I appreciate it. Some people learn, and some people don't. And that brings us to the next quality that often separates those who learn from their losses and those who don't. People often ask me what most determines if they will reach their potential. My answer: a teachable spirit.

What does it mean to be teachable? I define teachability as possessing the intentional attitude and behavior to keep learning and growing throughout life. Some people don't have that. Jazz trumpeter and bandleader Louis Armstrong described them when he said, "There are some people that if they don't know, you can't teach them." Some people want to be right, even when they aren't. And as a result, life is difficult for them. They never find the pathway of learning nor do they learn the lessons life offers to those with a teachable spirit.

> I define teachability as possessing the intentional attitude and behavior to keep learning and growing throughout life.

Futuristic author and speaker John Naisbitt said, "No one subject or set of subjects will serve you for a foreseeable future, let alone the rest of your life." In other words, even if you do know something well, it won't do everything for you. Living to your potential requires you to keep learning and expanding yourself. For that, you must have a teachable spirit. If you don't, you will come to the end of your potential long before you come to the end of your life.

> "No one subject or set of subjects will serve you for a foreseeable future, let alone the rest of your life."
> —John Naisbitt

If you want to be successful tomorrow, then you must be teachable today. What got you to where you are won't keep you here. And it certainly won't take you where you want to go. You need more than a great mind for learning. You need to have a great *heart* for learning. That's what a teachable spirit gives you.

Recently I read about a study conducted by Mark Murphy, founder and CEO of Leadership IQ. His organization tracked twenty thousand new hires over a three-year period and found that 46 percent of them failed (got fired, received poor performance reviews, or were written up) within the first eighteen months on the job. The main reason for the failure was not lack of technical competence. Weakness in that skill area was a problem for only one person in ten. Almost 90 percent of their problems were the result of attitude. The top reason for their failure was lack of teachability! Murphy writes that 26 percent of the people who failed weren't coachable. They lacked "the ability to accept and implement feedback from bosses, colleagues, customers, and others."[1]

The saddest thing about that is attitude is a choice. So is teachability. We choose whether we are open or closed to new ideas, new experiences, others' ideas, people's feedback, and willingness to change. We can choose the pathway to a better future by developing a teachable spirit, or we can sabotage that future by pretending that we know everything we need to move forward in life—which, by the way, is impossible for *anyone*!

Traits of a Teachable Person

If you desire to find the pathway from failure to success, you need to become a highly teachable person. How do you do that? By cultivating the following five traits:

1. Teachable People Have an Attitude Conducive to Learning

The attitude we carry with us in life sets the tone and direction for everything we do. In *Life's Greatest Lessons*, Hal Urban writes,

Golfers know that the success of their game is determined by how they approach the ball. Pilots know that the most critical part of landing a plane is in making the right approach. Lawyers know that how they approach the jury will be a determining factor in each case. Approaching means getting ready, taking the preliminary steps toward some type of achievement. The right approach to anything sets the stage for creating the results we hope for. In essence, our attitudes are the way we approach life. And the way we approach it will determine our success or failure.[2]

People with a teachable spirit approach each day as an opportunity for another learning experience. Their hearts are open. Their minds are alert for something new. Their attitudes are expectant. They know that success has less to do with possessing natural talent and more to do with choosing to learn.

When we are young, parents, teachers, and the educational system take primary responsibility for our learning. But that external impetus and responsibility for us to learn is gradually withdrawn over the course of our educational career. As we get older, and especially when we enter middle school and then move beyond it, a dividing line starts to appear between those who continue to be teachable and those who resist learning. The choice we make at that time is significant. We can choose to remain teachable and fuel our internal desire to intentionally grow. Or we can become indifferent to the opportunities that present themselves for us to keep learning.

Philip B. Crosby, the author of *Quality Is Free*, says that people can subconsciously retard their own growth because they come to rely on clichés and habits instead of cultivating a teachable spirit. "Once they reach the age of their own personal comfort with the world," says Crosby, "they stop learning and their mind runs on idle for the rest of their days. They may progress organizationally, they may be ambitious and eager, and they may even work night and day. But they learn no more."

Being teachable depends on two things: capacity and attitude. Our capacity may to some degree be set. But our attitude is totally our choice. We must proactively decide to embrace an attitude of teachability. Research conducted at Harvard and other universities confirms the importance of attitude to people's success. Attitude was found to be far more important than intelligence, education, special talent, or luck. In fact, it was concluded that up to 85 percent of success in life is due to attitude, while only 15 percent is due to ability.[3] Those findings are very consistent with those of Mark Murphy.

> Up to 85 percent of success in life is due to attitude, while only 15 percent is due to ability.

Only rarely have I known a teachable person whose approach toward life was negative. Most people with a teachable spirit and positive attitude don't allow negative ideas to hijack their thinking. Why? A closed mind does not open doors of opportunity. A scarcity mindset seldom creates abundance. A negative attitude rarely creates positive change.

If you have not cultivated a positive attitude and teachable spirit, I encourage you to fight for them. The sooner you do it, the better, because as age increases, our negative thoughts, bad habits, and weak character traits become more permanently ingrained. Getting older doesn't mean getting better. It just means you have less time in which to make the choice to become teachable. So make the choice to be teachable now. I know of no other way to keep learning in life.

2. Teachable People Possess a Beginner's Mind-set

As a young leader, I wanted to be successful, and I spent much of my time in the early years of my career searching for the keys to success. During that time, I attended a seminar where the facilitator asked us, "When you think of the most successful CEOs, entrepreneurs, and business owners, what qualities do you think they possess?"

We responded with words like *vision, intelligence, passion, determination,* and *work ethic.* Our facilitator agreed that all those things were important, but said the word that best describes top leaders is *teachability.* He went on to define *teachability* as the ability and willingness to learn and put into practice whatever was needed to accomplish our goals.

As a young leader I was surprised by his comment. I had thought successful people figured out what they needed to do, and then stuck with it. The people in my circle who had been most successful had an attitude of "been there, done that." They acted like they had it all figured out. As I grew older and gained more experience, I saw that their attitude got them only so far, and then they plateaued because they weren't growing. I also realized that I would never get to a place in life where I had everything figured out. I would always need to keep learning. I would always need to keep getting better. Successful people are continually learning new things.

What's the best way to do that? Have a beginner's mind-set. Erwin G. Hall observed, "An open mind is the beginning of self-discovery and growth. We can't learn anything new until we can admit that we don't already know everything." If you want to grow and learn, you must approach as many things as you can as a beginner, not an expert.

> "An open mind is the beginning of self-discovery and growth. We can't learn anything new until we can admit that we don't already know everything."
> —Erwin G. Hall

What do all beginners have in common? They know they don't know it all, and that shapes the way they approach things. In general, they're open and humble, lacking in the rigidity that often accompanies achievement. As Zen master Shunryu Suzuki wrote in the classic *Zen Mind, Beginner's Mind*, "In the beginner's mind there are many possibilities, but in the expert's mind there are few."

Most people enjoy being experts. In fact, some enjoy it so much and feel so uncomfortable as beginners that they work hard to avoid putting themselves in those situations. Others are more open and enjoy learning something new. When they are actually beginners, they find it easy to have a beginner's mind-set. But maintaining that teachability becomes more difficult as you learn more and achieve some degree of success. It's a challenge to remain receptive and open in every circumstance and situation over the course of time.

I try to maintain a beginner's mind-set, but I have to admit it's often difficult. To help me do it, I try to always keep the following three things in mind:

1. Everyone has something to teach me.
2. Every day I have something to learn.
3. Every time I learn something, I benefit.

The other thing I do is focus on asking questions. For too many years I concentrated on giving answers. As a young leader, I felt that was expected of me. But as soon as I started to get over my insecurity, I discovered that asking questions did more for my development than answering them, and the moment I intentionally asked questions and started listening, my personal and professional growth took off. Asking questions can do the same for you.

3. Teachable People Take Long, Hard Looks in the Mirror

Novelist James Thom remarked, "Probably the most honest, 'self-made' man ever was the one we heard say: 'I got to the top the hard way—fighting my own laziness and ignorance every step of the way.'" Can you relate to that statement? I certainly can. I'm known for writing and speaking on leadership, but the most difficult person I have ever led is me!

Becoming and remaining teachable requires people to honestly and openly evaluate themselves on a continual basis. Any time you face a challenge, loss, or problem, one of the first things you need to ask yourself is, "Am I the cause?" This is a key to teachability. If the answer is yes, then you need to be ready to make changes. Otherwise you're going to experience what one wit called "déjà-poo," the feeling you've been in this mess before.

When people refuse to look in the mirror and instead look to other people or situations to blame, they keep getting the same result over and over. Perhaps the best description of this that I've ever found—and the solution—is contained in a piece by Portia Nelson called "Autobiography in Five Short Chapters":

Chapter One

I walk down the street.
There is a deep hole in the sidewalk.
I fall in.
I am lost ... I am helpless.
It isn't my fault.
It takes forever to find my way out.

Chapter Two

I walk down the same street.
There is a deep hole in the sidewalk.
I pretend I don't see it.
I fall in again.
I can't believe I'm in the same place.
But it isn't my fault.
It still takes a long time to get out.

Chapter Three

I walk down the same street.
There is a deep hole in the sidewalk.
I see it is there.
I still fall in . . . it's a habit . . . but,
my eyes are open.
I know where I am.
It is my fault.
I get out immediately.

Chapter Four

I walk down the same street.
There is a deep hole in the sidewalk.
I walk around it.

Chapter Five

I walk down another street.

Recognizing your own part in your failings, seeking solutions (no matter how painful), and working hard to put them into place is teachability in action. And it leads to the ability to change, grow, and move forward in life.

Physician William Mayo prayed, "Lord, deliver me from the man who never makes a mistake, and also from the man who makes the same mistake twice." There's nothing wrong with making mistakes, but some people respond with encores. A teachable spirit will help to put a stop to that.

> "Lord, deliver me from the man who never makes a mistake, and also from the man who makes the same mistake twice."
> —William Mayo

4. Teachable People Encourage Others to Speak into Their Lives

One day a fox, a wolf, and a bear went hunting together. After each of them caught a deer, they discussed how to divide the spoils.

The bear asked the wolf how he thought it should be done. The wolf said everyone should get one deer. Suddenly the bear ate the wolf.

Then the bear asked the fox how he proposed to divvy things up. The fox offered the bear his deer and then said the bear ought to take the wolf's deer as well.

"Where did you get such wisdom?" asked the bear.

"From the wolf," replied the fox.

Unfortunately, most of us are too much like the bear. We don't like it when people speak the truth into our lives, and when someone has courage enough to speak up, we attack them. We need to react differently.

Teachable people need to surround themselves with people who know them well and who will lovingly, yet honestly, speak into their life. However, that can be a challenge—for many reasons. First, you must be willing to develop strong enough relationships with people that you can credibly ask them to speak into your life. Second, they must be courageous and honest enough to speak freely to you. And third, you must be willing to accept their feedback and criticism without defending yourself. Otherwise, you'll only receive it once!

That process becomes further complicated if you are highly successful. When you are influential and highly respected, people tend to tell you what you want to hear, not what you *need* to hear. They are seeking your approval, or they flatter you. Unfortunately, that creates a gap between what you hear and reality. If you find yourself in that situation, you will need to work extra hard to get the people close to you to speak honesty into your life. And you will have to become highly intentional in observing and listening.

Everybody needs someone who is willing to speak into his life. Ideally, it should be someone who is above you organizationally or ahead of you experientially. When I was leading a large church in San Diego, I invited feedback and criticism from Steve Babby, who oversaw the leaders of dozens of churches in Southern California. At least once a year I'd ask Steve to point out anything he thought I was doing that was wrong or weaknesses in my leadership that he believed might have me headed for trouble. After a couple of years of this, Steve once said, "John, you are the most successful person I work with, yet you are the *only* one who invites criticism. Why?"

"I don't trust anyone with power that can't be checked," I answered. "Especially me."

Writer Peter M. Leschak asserted, "All of us are watchers—of television, of time clocks, of traffic on the freeway—but few are observers. Everyone is looking, not many are seeing." Look for clues that you may be off track, and ask people to verify your suspicions. They will be more likely to speak freely if you've brought up your deficiency first.

I have to admit, listening is a learned skill in my life. Talking is much more natural for me. My mother used to tell everyone, "At six months John started talking and he never stopped." It's true. I never run out of words to say. I like to set the tone. I like to entertain. I like to teach and mentor. But talking isn't learning. Listening is. Columnist Doug Larson said, "Wisdom is the reward you get for a lifetime of listening when you would have preferred to talk." I try to keep that in mind. If you're a talker, you should, too.

> "Wisdom is the reward you get for a lifetime of listening when you would have preferred to talk."
> —Doug Larson

5. Teachable People Learn Something New Every Day

The secret to any person's success can be found in his or her daily agenda. People grow and improve, not by huge leaps and bounds, but by small, incremental changes. Children's advocate Marian Wright Edelman said, "We must not, in trying to think about how we can make a big difference, ignore the small daily differences we can make which, over time, add up to big differences that we often cannot foresee." She understands that progress comes day by day, inch by inch.

Teachable people try to leverage this truth by learning something new every day. A single day is enough to make us a little larger or a little smaller. Several single days strung together will make us a lot larger or a lot smaller. If we do that every day, day upon day, there is great power for change. Author and motivational speaker Dennis P. Kimbro gives insight into this in a piece he wrote years ago:

I am your constant companion. I am your greatest helper or heaviest burden. I will push you onward, or drag you down to failure. I am completely at your command. Half of the things you do, you might just as well turn over to me, and I will be able to do them quickly and correctly. I am easily managed—you must merely be firm with me. Show me exactly how you want something done and after a few lessons, I will do it automatically. I am the servant of all great men; and alas, of all failures, as well. Those who are failures, I have made failures. Those who are great, I have made great. I am not a machine, though I work with all the precision of a machine, plus the intelligence of a man. You may run me for profit, or run me for ruin—it makes no difference to me. Take me, train me, be firm with me, and I will place the world at your feet. Be easy with me and I will destroy you. Who am I? I am a habit.[4]

The habits you practice every day will make you or break you, just as Kimbro suggests. If you want to become a teachable person who learns from losses, then make learning your daily habit. It may not change your life in a day. But it will change your days for life.

Daily Practices to Become More Teachable

If you believe in the idea of trying to learn something new every day, but you don't know the best way to go about it, then I recommend that you engage in the following three practices every day.

1. Preparation

If you want to be ready to meet whatever challenges you're going to face on a given day and learn from them, you need to be prepared. That means working in advance—every day. As my old mentor John

> "When opportunity comes, it's too late to prepare."
> —John Wooden

Wooden used to say, "When opportunity comes, it's too late to prepare."

How do I go about preparing for my day so that I can learn from it? I start each morning by looking at my schedule. As I review my commitments for the day, I ask myself some questions:

- Where are the potential learning moments for today?
- Who will I meet and what can I ask them?
- What will I experience and what might I be able to learn from it?

By looking for the probable teaching moments and preparing for them, I make learning possible.

The first time I met with Coach Wooden, I spent hours in preparation. I wrote pages of questions to ask him. After our first few hours in which he patiently answered my questions, I asked him if we could meet again in the future. I will never forget his answer. He said, "Yes, John, we can meet again. I can tell you will always be prepared for our time together." What a great compliment. That was the beginning of many wonderful meetings. Every time I left this wise man, I felt fulfilled by what I had learned.

You don't have to spend hours in preparation every day, though you may sometimes have things on your schedule that would warrant such preparation. Just plan to spend a few minutes each morning or the evening before thinking through what your day will be like and where the greatest potential opportunities lie for you to learn. You will be amazed by how often you can improve yourself just drawing on the people and experiences that are part of your daily life.

2. Contemplation

Time alone is essential to learning. Contemplation allows people to observe and reflect on the occurrences of their lives and derive meaning from them. Stopping and thinking allows us to gain perspective on both the successes and failures of our day so that we can find the lessons within them. It also enables you to plan how you can improve in the future.

It's good to remember that there's much to learn from negative experiences. In science, mistakes always precede discoveries. It is impossible to make discoveries without an accumulation of errors. To a scientist, a mistake is not failure—it's feedback. Using that feedback, a scientist can ask not just "What happened?" but also "What does it mean?" That comes from using critical thinking skills. Without them, we miss the meaning of the occurrences in our lives.

> It's good to remember that there's much to learn from negative experiences. In science, mistakes always precede discoveries.

When the lessons we learn come from mistakes, we must first determine if the mistake was due to ignorance or stupidity. *Ignorance* means we didn't have the necessary information; *stupidity* means we had the necessary information but misused it.

As you spend time in contemplation, ask yourself questions like these:

- What can I learn from what I read today?
- What can I learn from what I saw today?
- What can I learn from what I heard today?
- What can I learn from what I experienced today?

- What can I learn from what I did wrong today?
- What can I learn from whom I met today?
- What can I learn from what I discussed today?

I recommend that you set aside thirty minutes at the end of every day to think about the preceding twenty-four hours, contemplating what occurred and what you can learn from it. Not only will that help you to remain teachable, but you will also learn something every day because of the process.

3. Application

The true value of teachability comes when we take something that we learn and apply it. We can learn a lot from our mistakes if we remain teachable. Not everyone does that. When people make mistakes, they generally do one of three things in response to them: They resolve to never make another mistake, which is impossible. They allow their mistake to make them into cowards, which is foolish. Or they make up their minds to learn from their mistake and apply the lesson to their lives, which is profitable.

Other times we learn from the positives and apply those lessons. Recently, my assistant, Linda Eggers, asked me if I wanted to see a list of all the books I had written. The big surprise to me was the number of books: seventy-one! I never dreamed that would be possible. I remember when I wanted to write my first book. The task was overwhelming. I chipped away at it for over a year, and even then I was able to eke out only 120 pages. I could hardly believe it.

What was the lesson I learned from that? If you keep focused on the task at hand and you keep working at it, day after day, week after week, year after year, you can accomplish much. But there was also another lesson. The only reason I was able to write so many books was that I take a similarly disciplined approach to learning. I try to learn something new every day. And because I do that, the pool of what I'm learning keeps growing, not diminishing. A friend recently asked me how many more books I want to write. I don't have a specific number. The answer will be determined by whether I remain teachable and keep applying what I discover. As long as I'm still learning, I will continue to have something to say.

Teachability under Fire

Some people may be tempted to think that teachability is for people with advantages and that it's more difficult for people who are under-privileged, facing adversity, or suffering pain to be teachable. But I don't think that's true. I believe teachability is an attitude, a mind-set that teachable people carry with them wherever they go and whatever they experience.

A great example of this can be found in the life of Richard Wurm-brand, who was born in Romania in 1909. As a young man, he went into business. By the time he was twenty-five, he had made a lot of money and was living the high life. When he was twenty-seven, he contracted tuberculosis. His poor health prompted him to reexam-ine his life, and he became a person of strong faith. So did his wife a short time later. A few years after that, Wurmbrand felt compelled to become a minister.

During World War II, Romania suffered under the Nazis and Sovi-ets. Wurmbrand recalled,

As the war progressed, many of the Christian minorities...
were massacred or driven into concentration camps with the

Jews. All of my wife's family were carried off—she never saw them again. I was arrested by the Fascists on three occasions; tried, interrogated, beaten, and imprisoned. So I was well prepared for what was to come under the Communists.[5]

As the end of the war neared, Russian troops poured into Romania and it fell under Communist rule. The persecution of Christians, especially pastors, became commonplace. In February 1948, Wurmbrand was arrested. "I was walking alone down a street in Bucharest," he recalled, "when a black Ford car braked sharply beside me and two men jumped out. They seized my arms and thrust me into the back seat, while a third man beside the driver kept me covered with a pistol."[6]

The Communist secret police had taken him, accusing him of spying for the West. They left him alone for months at a time. At other times he was tortured and questioned. Often they tried to get him to confess to crimes he had not committed. At other times they tried to get him to implicate other "conspirators." Wurmbrand was willing to inform on himself, but never on others. He was put in solitary confinement for three years with nothing to read and no writing materials. He was placed in a cupboardlike area with spikes on the walls for days at a time. In all, he spent fourteen years in various Communist prisons. After he finally got out and moved to the West, he founded Voice of the Martyrs, a nonprofit organization dedicated to helping persecuted Christians.

During his imprisonment, Wurmbrand made it his goal to learn. His particular focus was on his spiritual development. But he also tried to pass on his teachable spirit to others while incarcerated. Once when a fellow prisoner was being led away to a punishment cell where many prisoners had died, Wurmbrand, who had previously been put in the same cell, said to the man, "When you come back, tell us what you have learned."

Why would Wurmbrand do that? He was trying to remind the man to maintain a teachable spirit so that he would have hope and keep on living.

The desire to learn is a great motivation to keep on living, whether you are a child first exploring the world, a worker, a prisoner, or an elderly person in the December of life. It keeps us young and alive and full of hope. That is the power of remaining teachable.

8

Adversity: The Catalyst for Learning

Marshall Taylor was born into a financially struggling family in Indianapolis, Indiana, in 1878. His grandfather had been a slave. His father had fought for the Union in the Civil War, and was working as a coachman for a wealthy family named the Southards when Marshall was born. As a young boy, Marshall sometimes accompanied his father to his job and exercised the horses.

When Marshall was thirteen years old, the Southards moved to Chicago. They wanted to take young Marshall with them, because he had become such good friends with their son, who was the same age. In fact, Marshall had spent so much time with the Southards that he was treated like a member of their family. But the Taylors didn't want to move. And Marshall's mother couldn't stand the thought of having her son leave her. So Marshall stayed put, and overnight his life changed from advantage to adversity. He later said, "I was dropped from the happy life of a 'millionaire kid' to that of a common errand boy, all within a few weeks."[1]

Strong Work Ethic

Marshall immediately began looking for ways to make money. The Southards had given him a bicycle, so he began using it to deliver papers. For entertainment, he also taught himself how to do tricks with the bicycle. When the owners of a local bicycle shop learned about this ability, they hired Marshall. They put him in a military-style uniform and had him do tricks and stunts in front of their shop. Because of the uniform, the locals started calling him "Major."

This was in the early 1890s, a time when bicycles were all the rage. At the turn of the century, the United States had 75 million people and only 5,000 cars, but more than 20 million bicycles.[2] And the biggest and most popular sport in America and Europe was bicycle racing.[3] People loved the races and turned out by the tens of thousands to see them, the way that people watch football and soccer today.

There were all kinds of bicycle races. Some were short sprints of a fraction of a mile. Others were longer distances. A few were multiday endurance contests where racers slept for maybe an hour for every eight hours racing. These long races of exhausted riders often resulted in injuries and occasionally even in deaths. Thousands of spectators watched the races in major cities across America and Europe. And some professional racers made a great living—four times as much as pro baseball players.[4]

Trying to make the most of racing's popularity to promote their bicycle shop, one of the shop owners who employed Marshall entered him in a ten-mile race.

"I know you can't go the full distance," he told the nervous Marshall, "but just ride up the road a little way, it will please the crowd, and you can come back as soon as you get tired."[5]

What the shop owner didn't know was that Marshall cycled to and from work every day—twenty-five miles in each direction. The boy took off, and much to his employer's shock and pleasure, not only did he finish the race, but he won! Though the race exhausted him to the point of collapse, he beat the other experienced adult racers by a six-second margin. And he was only thirteen years old!

Only the Start

That day was the beginning of an exceptional racing career for Marshall Taylor. It was also the beginning of a life of even greater adversity. Many of the local racers didn't like being beaten by someone who wasn't white. As a result, they made it very difficult for him. He was regularly threatened. A group of white riders made sure he would not be allowed to join any of the local riding clubs. And eventually they even had him barred from competing in the local races.

They suspected that Marshall was better than they were. When he was seventeen, he proved it. A friend and mentor managed to get Marshall accepted into what would essentially be an exhibition, since none of his results would be official. Marshall rode in a one mile race and beat the track by more than eight seconds. Then he completed the one-fifth-mile race and beat the world record time.

Knowing that he would never be accepted in Indianapolis, Marshall moved to Massachusetts, choosing the state because its delegation of the League of American Wheelmen was the only one to vote unanimously *not* to prohibit black members at a previous meeting. He competed successfully there, but many people still refused to accept him. He was repeatedly threatened. Racers would work together to box him in or try to harm him. After Marshall won one race, another cyclist beat him and nearly choked him to death. And when Marshall decided to go south to train one winter and set up in Savannah, Georgia, he hadn't been there long before he received the following letter:

Dear Mr. Taylor,

    If you don't leave here before 48 hours, you will be sorry. We mean business—clear out if you value your life.

White Racers

A crude skull and crossbones had been scribbled at the bottom of the letter.[6] Marshall headed back north.

Marshall's career was remarkable. The Black Cyclone, as he was called, turned professional while still a teenager. Before turning twenty, he set seven world records. He won twenty-nine of the forty-nine races he entered. And he won the world championship of cycling in 1899. He retired in 1910 at the age of thirty-two.

Sadly, Marshall was wiped out financially by the stock market crash and the great depression. He died a pauper in 1932. And his story of courage in overcoming adversity was forgotten by many. But not by his family. His granddaughter, Jan Brown, says, "The most breathtaking part of his story is his resistance to the limitations that others would have had for him. . . . The fact that he retained the focus and sense of spirit necessary to define and pursue his own goals is itself a prize. The fact that he achieved them, and did so in such a stirring way, is pure icing on the cake."[7]

The *If* Factor

Writer and professor Robertson Davies said, "Extraordinary people survive under the most terrible circumstances and then become more extraordinary because of it." That was certainly true of Marshall Taylor. The pain of adversity never leaves us the same. It is the catalyst for change. In Marshall's case, he didn't become bitter. He just worked harder. When he discovered that his competitors were going to try to hurt him during races, he learned to get out in front of them and stay there! He used adversity to make himself smarter—and better.

> "Extraordinary people survive under the most terrible circumstances and then become more extraordinary because of it."
> —*Robertson Davies*

I believe that one of the times people change is when they hurt enough that they have to. Adversity causes pain and is a prompt for change. Most of the time we don't choose our adversity, but all the time we can choose our response to it. *If* we respond positively to difficulties, the outcome will be potentially positive. *If* we respond negatively to our difficulties, the outcome will be potentially negative. That's why I call our response "the if factor."

There's a story about a young woman who complained to her father about her life and how hard things were for her. The adversity of life was overwhelming her, and she wanted to give up.

As he listened, her father filled three pots with water and brought them to a boil on the stove. Into the first he put carrot slices, into the second he put eggs, and into the third he put ground coffee beans. He let them simmer for a few minutes and then placed the carrots, eggs, and coffee before her in three containers.

"What do you see?" he asked.

"Carrots, eggs, and coffee," she replied.

He asked her to feel the carrots. She picked up a piece and it squished between her fingers. He then asked her to examine an egg. She picked one up, broke the shell, and saw the hard-boiled egg inside it. Finally, he asked her to sip the coffee. She smiled, as she tasted its rich flavor.

"So what does it mean?" she asked.

"Each ingredient was subjected to the same thing—boiling water—but each reacted differently. The carrots went in hard. But after they were in the boiling water, they became soft. The egg was fragile with a thin outer shell and a liquid interior. But it became hardened. The ground coffee beans changed little. But they changed the water for the better.

"Which are you," he asked. "When you face adversity, how do you respond? Are you a carrot, an egg, or a coffee bean?"

Life is filled with adversity. We can be squashed by it. We can allow it to make us hard. Or we can make the best of it, improving the situation. As British prime minister Winston Churchill noted, "I have derived continued benefit from criticism at all periods of my life, and I do not remember any time when I was ever short of it." Since you will face adversity, why not make the best of it?

The Advantages of Adversity

Adversity is a catalyst for learning. It can actually create advantages for you *if* you face it with the right mind-set. It all depends on how you respond to it. Here's what I mean:

1. Adversity Introduces Us to Ourselves If We Want to Know Ourselves

Adversity always gets our attention. We can't ignore it. It causes us to stop and look at our situation. And at ourselves if we have the courage. Adversity is an opportunity for self-discovery. As the great Egyptian leader Anwar el-Sadat said, "Great suffering builds up a human being and puts him within the reach of self-knowledge." This I believe is true—if we embrace it that way.

> Adversity is an opportunity for self-discovery.

Unfortunately, many people choose to hide during times of adversity. They build walls, close their eyes, run away, medicate themselves, or do whatever they must to avoid dealing with the reality of the situation. They are like Sergeant Schulz in the old TV comedy *Hogan's Heroes*. Anytime something happens that they don't want to acknowledge, they say, "I know nothing. I see nothing." If that is your response to adversity, you will never understand the situation or yourself.

One of my favorite books is *As a Man Thinketh* by James Allen. My father required me to read it when I was in junior high school. One of the ideas that left the strongest impression on me as a youth was this: "Circumstance does not make the man; it reveals him to himself." That is true, but only *if* you allow it to.

Speaker Tony Robbins contrasts the differences between one person who wins the lottery and another who is paralyzed from the neck down in an accident. Who does he say is happiest after three years? The paralyzed person. Why? The lottery winner hopes for his life to change but bases it on circumstances. In contrast, the paralyzed person is introduced to himself through adversity. He rises to challenges he never knew he could face. And he comes to appreciate the good things in his life, including relationships, as he never did before.

"In the end," says Robbins, "when someone looks at their life and thinks about what makes them happy, they usually think about the people they love, and the challenges they faced and overcame, as defining their inner strength. These things are what they're proud of and what they want to remember."

Adversity has introduced me to myself in many times during my lifetime. It has opened my eyes. It has plumbed the depths of my heart. It has tested my strength. And it has taught me a lot. Here are a few of the lessons I've learned:

- When I have gotten off track and am seemingly lost, I have learned that the road to success is not always a road.
- When I have been exhausted and frustrated, I have learned that trying times are not the time to stop trying.
- When I have been discouraged with my progress, I have learned not to let what I was doing get to me before I got to it.
- When I have failed, I have learned that I will not be judged by the number of times I have failed but by the number of times I succeed.

Adversity has introduced me to tenacity, creativity, focus, and many other positive things that have helped me to like myself better. Novelist and songwriter Samuel Lover asserted, "Circumstances are the rulers of the weak; but they are the instruments of the wise." If I respond negatively to my circumstances, they will keep me enslaved to them. If I respond wisely, my circumstances will serve me.

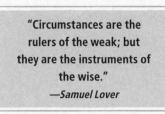

"Circumstances are the rulers of the weak; but they are the instruments of the wise."
—Samuel Lover

2. Adversity Is a Better Teacher Than Success If We Want to Learn from Adversity

Adversity comes to us as a teaching tool. You've probably heard the saying, "When the pupil is ready the teacher will come." That is not necessarily true. With adversity, the teacher will come whether the pupil is ready or not. Those who are ready learn from the teacher. Those who are not don't learn.

Philosopher and author Emmet Fox said, "It is the Law that many difficulties that can come to you at any time, no matter what they are, must be exactly what you need at the moment, to enable you to take the next step forward by overcoming them. The only real misfortune, the only real tragedy comes when we suffer without learning the lesson." The key to avoiding that tragedy is *wanting* to learn from life's difficulties.

One of the things I enjoy most about taking trips with family is the time we get talking together. Over the years, Margaret and I have enjoyed many wonderful trips with my brother Larry and his wife, Anita. We dine together. We visit the sites. We share laughter and sometimes tears. It's fantastic to have so many memories from so many places in the world with people we love.

Not long ago we spent a week in Vienna, Austria. What a wonderful city, filled with history and musical influences. One night we sat in a café, where I shared with Larry and Anita that I was writing this book and asked for their thoughts. After hearing the premise of the book, Larry immediately quoted the following poem by Robert Browning Hamilton, which he learned as a boy:

I walked a mile with pleasure;
She chatted all the way,
But left me none the wiser,
With all she had to say.

I walked a mile with sorrow;
And never a word said she,
But oh the things I learned from her,
When sorrow walked with me.[8]

Oprah Winfrey's advice to "turn your wounds into wisdom" can come true for us only *if* we want to learn from our wounds. It requires

> "Turn your wounds into wisdom."
> —Oprah Winfrey

the right mind-set and a deliberate intention to find the lesson in the loss. If we don't embrace those things, then all we end up with is the scars.

3. Adversity Opens Doors for New Opportunities If We Want to Learn from It

One of the greatest lessons I've learned as a leader is that adversity is often the door to opportunity. Good entrepreneurs know this instinctively, but most people have been trained to see adversity the wrong way. As speaker and cofounder of the Rich Dad Company, Kim Kiyosaki, observed, "Most of us are taught, beginning in kindergarten, that mistakes are bad. How often did you hear, 'Don't make a mistake!' In reality, the way we learn is by *making* mistakes. A mistake simply shows you something you didn't know. Once you make the mistake, then you know it. Think about the first time you touched a hot stove (the mistake). From making that mistake, you learned that if you touch a hot stove you get burned. A mistake isn't bad; it's there to teach you something."

When many people face adversity, they let it get them down. Instead, they need to look for the benefit or opportunity. One of my favorite examples of this occurred with Proctor and Gamble back in the 1870s. One day at the factory, an employee went to lunch and forgot to turn off the machinery that was mixing the soap. When he returned, the soap had increased in volume because air had been whipped into it. What a mistake! What should he do? He didn't want to throw it out, so he poured it into the frames, and it was cut, packaged, and shipped, even though he had ruined it.

A few weeks later, the company began receiving letters from customers asking for more orders of the soap that floated. Why? The soap was used in factories. At the end of their shift, factory workers washed at vats of standing water that became murky. Bars of soap that floated were easier to find when dropped. A manufacturing mistake led to an opportunity, the creation of Ivory soap, which is still sold today, more than one hundred years later.

You don't have to be a businessperson or entrepreneur to take advantage of the opportunities brought about by adversity. For example, in the weeks following the terrorist attacks of September 11, 2001, in New York City, Rudy Guiliani and other New Yorkers reminded everyone that New York was open for business, because few people were visiting the city. Margaret and I saw that as an opportunity and went to New York for a week. Imagine how much fun we had as we easily got tickets to all the best Broadway shows and ate at any restaurant we wanted. It was a once-in-a-lifetime trip!

As I write this book, the economies in America and in many other places around the world are not doing well. However, within the financial freefall many opportunities are surfacing. Business history is filled with examples of products and services that were launched during difficult recessions:

- Boeing's 707 airliner (1957)
- FedEx (1973)
- Microsoft's MS-DOS (1981)
- Apple's iPod (2001)

As Muriel "Mickie" Siebert, the First Woman of Finance, said, "Any significant change in business is an opportunity for a new business."

Are you seeing the opportunities?

> "Any significant change in business is an opportunity for a new business."
> —*Muriel "Mickie" Siebert*

Are you looking for ways to take advantage of them? Real estate prices are down: there is an opportunity. Interest rates are down: that brings opportunities. Business needs are changing; that provides a wealth of opportunities. Every adversity brings an advantage. Are you trying to make the most of it? Or are you letting adversity get you down?

4. Adversity Can Signal a Coming Positive Transition If We Respond Correctly to It

In 1915, the people of Coffee City, Alabama, were devastated after their cotton crop was destroyed by boll weevils. The area's entire economy was built on cotton. What would they do? Scientist George Washington Carver suggested that local farmers grow peanuts.

When the crop came in, Carver was able to show how peanuts could be used to create chemicals needed to make soap, ink, plastics, and cosmetics. It opened up the economy to new crops, new ideas, and a brighter future. Today peanuts are still a vital crop in the southern United States. How fortunate it was for everyone that Carver has seen the opportunity for a transition that adversity had provided.

In 1996, I founded EQUIP, a nonprofit organization that exists to train leaders internationally. So far we have trained more than 5 million leaders in 173 countries. But EQUIP also works to assist international leaders in times of crisis. Why? Because we believe that crises frequently give leaders the opportunity to learn, make positive changes, and create transitions to help their people. For example, when many of Poland's leaders were killed in a plane crash several years ago, leaders from EQUIP traveled to Poland, because we knew that the response of leaders during negative transitions determines the response of the people.

The life of a successful person is comprised of one transition after another. Being static isn't an option in life. Time is always moving forward. We can't stop it, nor can we stop its effects. We need to make changes, and adversity can often be the catalyst. James Allen wrote, "Let a person rejoice when he is confronted with obstacles, for it means that he has reached the end of some particular line of indifference or folly, and is now called upon to summon up all his energy and intelligence in order to extricate himself, and to find a better way; that the powers within him are crying out for greater freedom, for enlarged exercise and scope."

5. Adversity Brings Profit as Well as Pain If We Expect It and Plan for It

In the movie *Black Hawk Down* a vehicle filled with wounded American soldiers lurches to a stop in the middle of a street where Somali bullets are flying in every direction. The officer in charge tells a soldier to get in and start driving.

"I can't," says the soldier. "I'm shot."

"We're all shot," responds the officer. "Get in and drive!"

In life we should all expect pain. It's a part of life. It's a part of loss. The question is, are you going to let it stop you from doing what you want and need to do?

No one ever says, "Go for the silver." Athletes, coaches, and fans always say, "Go for the gold!" Why? Because gold represents the best. If you're going to endure the pain it takes to compete, why not compete to win?

Successful people expect to experience pain when they face adversity. They plan for it. And by planning for it, they set themselves up to benefit from it. Fred Smith once said, "I listened to Bob Richards, the Olympic gold medalist, interview younger Olympian winners of the

gold. He asked them, 'What did you do when you began to hurt?'"
Fred points out that none of the Olympians were surprised by the question. They expected pain, and they had
a strategy for dealing with it. As Bob
Richards summed up, "You never win
the gold without hurting."

> **"You never win the gold without hurting."**
> —*Bob Richards*

An article by Amy Wilkinson in *USA Today* described the entrepreneurial spirit of America, which can be traced back to its begin-
nings and came to fruition during the American Revolution. Wilkinson
wrote:

> The handful of individuals who founded the USA were no
> strangers to risk and innovation. George Washington started
> one of the largest whiskey distilleries in the new nation. Ben-
> jamin Franklin was an inventor, and Thomas Jefferson an
> architect.
>
> But these entrepreneurs made their riskiest investment [in
> 1776] when they laid the foundations for a democratic nation
> that endured despite formidable odds. In doing so, they set a
> precedent for daring and imagination that would come to define
> the American Dream.[9]

The Founding Fathers knew that they would face adversity as they
rebelled against England. They knew they would suffer pain. But
because they were prepared for it, they also were able to reap benefits
from it. The citizens of the United States continue to reap those benefits. Wilkinson sums up the lesson by quoting PayPal cofounder Peter
Thiel, who said, "The lesson people learned was that things are hard
but if you really work at it, you can get it to work." This is a lesson that
all successful people learn and put into practice.

6. Adversity Writes Our Story and If Our Response Is Right, the Story Will Be Good

Some people treat adversity as a stepping-stone, others as a tombstone. The difference in the way they approach it depends on how they see it. Performance psychologist Jim Loehr says, "Champions have taught us how to take an experience and essentially write the story of its effect. If you see a failure as an opportunity to learn and get better, it will be. If you perceive it as a mortal blow, it will be. In that way, the power of the story is more important than the experience itself."

Golf, which is a game of high highs and low lows, provides great examples of this. Some golfers bounce back from adversity, and their actions write a great story. Others crumble. For example, in 1982, when he was forty-six years old, Jack Nicklaus lost the U.S. Open after Tom Watson chipped in and took the lead. Most people thought Nicklaus was done. But he won the Masters four years later. Contrast that with Tony Jacklin, who lost the 1972 British Open by three, putting from close range after Lee Trevino's chip-in. Jacklin later said, "I had the heart ripped out of me. I was never the same."

If you respond right to adversity, you see it as something that can help you to become better than you were before. I read a poem years ago by James Casey called "Climb the Steep." The first stanza says,

> For every hill I've had to climb
> For every rock that bruised my feet
> For all the blood and sweat and grime
> For blinding storms and burning heat
> My heart sings but a grateful song
> These were the things that made me strong[10]

What kind of story will adversity write in your life? Will it be like Nicklaus's or like Jacklin's? I hope yours will be positive. Adversity without triumph is not inspiring; it's depressing. Adversity without growth is not encouraging; it's discouraging. The great potential story in adversity is one of hope and success. Adversity is everyone's, but the story you write with your life is yours alone. Everyone gets a chance to be the hero in a potentially great story. Some step up to that role and some don't. The choice is yours.

> Adversity is everyone's, but the story you write with your life is yours alone.

As you consider whether you will allow adversity to become a catalyst for learning in your life, consider this Franciscan blessing:

May God bless you with discomfort at easy answers, half truths, and superficial relationships, so that you may live deep within your heart.

May God bless you with anger at injustice, oppression, and exploitation of people, so that you may work for justice, freedom, and peace.

May God bless you with tears to shed for those who suffer from pain, rejection, starvation, and war, so that you may reach out your hand to comfort them and turn their pain to joy.

And may God bless you with enough foolishness to believe that you can make a difference in this world, so that you can do what others claim cannot be done.

That is my prayer for myself, and it is also my hope for you.

9

Problems: Opportunities for Learning

Whenever I feel like problems are going to overwhelm me, and I'm in danger of getting discouraged, I pull out and read a story I came across years ago. It's an account of what would happen today if Noah tried to build the Ark.

And the Lord spoke to Noah and said, "In six months I'm going to make it rain until the whole earth is covered with water and all the evil people are destroyed. But I want to save a few good people, and two of every kind of living thing on the planet. I am ordering you to build me an Ark." And in a flash of lightning he delivered the specifications for an Ark.

"Okay," said Noah, trembling in fear and fumbling with the blueprints.

"Six months, and it starts to rain," thundered the Lord. "You'd better have my Ark completed, or you can learn how to swim for a very long time."

And six months passed. The skies began to cloud up and rain began to fall. The Lord saw that Noah was sitting in his front yard weeping. And there was no Ark.

"Noah," shouted the Lord, "where is my Ark?" A lightning bolt crashed into the ground next to Noah.

"Lord, please forgive me!" begged Noah. "I did my best. But there were big problems. First I had to get a building permit for the Ark construction project, and your plans didn't meet code. So I had to hire an engineer to redraw the plans. Then I got into a big fight over whether or not the Ark needed a fire sprinkler system. My neighbors objected, claiming I was violating zoning by building the Ark in my front yard, so I had to get a variance from the city planning commission.

"Then I had a big problem getting enough wood for the Ark because there was a ban on cutting trees to save the spotted owl. I had to convince U.S. Fish and Wildlife that I needed the wood to save the owls. But they wouldn't let me catch any owls. So no owls.

"Then the carpenters formed a union and went out on strike. I had to negotiate a settlement with the National Labor Relations Board before anyone would pick up a saw or a hammer. Now we have sixteen carpenters on the boat, and still no owls.

"Then I started gathering up animals, and got sued by an animal rights group. They objected to my taking only two of each kind. Just when I got the suit dismissed, the EPA notified me that I couldn't complete the Ark without filing an environmental impact statement on your proposed flood. They didn't take kindly to the idea that they had no jurisdiction over the conduct of a Supreme Being. Then the Army Corps of Engineers wanted a map of the proposed new flood plain. I sent them a globe.

"Right now I'm still trying to resolve a complaint from the Equal Employment Opportunity Commission over how many people I'm supposed to hire, the IRS has seized all my assets claiming I'm trying to avoid paying taxes by leaving the country, and I just got a notice from the state about owing some kind of use tax. I really don't think I can finish your Ark for at least another five years!"

The sky began to clear. The sun began to shine. A rainbow arched across the sky. Noah looked up and smiled. "You mean you're not going to destroy the earth?" he asked hopefully.

"No," said the Lord sadly, "Government already has."[1]

My Own Flood of Problems

I just love that story because it's so outrageous. Nobody could face those kinds of problems in real life, right? Well, you may be surprised to learn that I had my own leadership experience that felt a lot like Noah's when I was the leader of a church in La Mesa, California. I arrived and took over leadership in 1981, but it didn't take me long to realize we had two major problems: we were in a poor location, and we would soon outgrow our outdated facilities.

I knew I needed to do something, so I started moving the people in the direction of change. And despite people's emotional attachment to the location and facility, in 1983 they voted to relocate. I had built buildings in my previous two posts and relocated the people in one of those ventures, so I figured I knew what lay ahead. But was I wrong. This turned out to be my single greatest leadership challenge, and the source of problem after problem.

Imagine our excitement when we bought the plot of land: 130

acres for $1.8 million. That was a challenge, but it wasn't anything we couldn't overcome. With great anticipation and hope, we started planning. The first problem arose because of where we wanted to situate our main building, right on top of the ridge of the property's hill. That way it would have a wonderful view of the area, and people would be aware of us in the community. But local officials said that would be too intrusive to the community. That was a disappointment, but we didn't want to alienate our neighbors, so we adjusted.

If you want to build in California, you have to pay for environmental studies. That just comes with the territory. So we did. In the course of that study, it was discovered that one pair of California black-tailed gnatcatchers sometimes inhabited the plot of land. You'd expect there to be animals on undeveloped land, so that didn't seem like a big deal. There was only one problem: that is an endangered bird species. It was decided that during their six-month breeding period we would not be allowed to do anything that would disturb them. That greatly affected our potential building times.

Then it was discovered that coastal sage grew on the land. Guess what? That was another problem. We were told that we would not be allowed to build anywhere that the sage grew. So we changed the plans for our building site—again.

We changed them again when we learned that State Route 94 was going to be extended. Guess where? Through our proposed building site. Again we moved it.

Then somebody found a blackened stone on the property. We didn't think that was unusual. Before the San Diego area was highly developed, people used to camp and ride dirt bikes all over the eastern part of the county. But there was a problem: an expert believed this stone might have been the remains of a cooking hearth used by the area's inhabitants two thousand years ago. We had to pay $120,000 for an archeological dig.

Because the cost of putting up a building was going to be so high, we decided to sell a section of the land that fronted the state highway to generate funds. This would do much to help with the cost of our building. But there was a problem. The county declared that the section of land we intended to sell had to be declared open space because of another bird, Bell's vireo.

When we realized that the topography of the land was going to make parking difficult, we purchased eight more acres at the cost of $250,000. Although it was expensive, we knew this would provide us room for six hundred more parking spaces. But there was a problem. The county decided that piece of land needed to be used for "environmental connectivity" for wildlife. There went another quarter million dollars.

At this point, we had spent millions of dollars and nearly a decade trying to make our way through the bureaucratic red tape, and we still didn't have our building permit! Our plan was to develop twenty-five of the 138 acres we had purchased. But guess what? There was a problem. Officials decided that we would be doing too much damage to the environment if we developed those acres and left *only* 113 acres for the wildlife. To mitigate the damage, we were required to buy another twenty-five acres in the mountains for $150,000 and turn over the deed for that land to an environmental trust.

Then—and only then—after twelve long years, did we receive approval from the County Board of Supervisors for a *permit*. Finally we could begin site work. By this time, my successor, Jim Garlow, had taken over the project. But guess what? We weren't out of the woods yet. We still had more problems.

We always knew there was granite on the property, and had projected

$38,000 for blasting. But it wasn't until they started moving dirt that it was discovered that it was blue granite, which is six times stronger than concrete; the cost of blasting was ten times what was planned. While two required water pipes were being installed on the property, workers hit more blue granite; that added another $192,000 to the cost and extended the construction process by two and a half years.

During construction, it was decided that the road running along the edge of the property was to be turned into a freeway. San Diego County agreed to pay $1 million toward the construction and the church was ordered to pay $1.1 million. And due to changing construction require- ments related to earthquake safety, the amount of steel and concrete in one of the buildings was increased by an additional $856,000.

Success at last! The run of problems looked like they would never end. But *finally* on the weekend of April 15–16, 2000, at Jim's invita- tion, I walked into the new facility along with more than five thousand people and we all celebrated. It had taken a total of seventeen years and millions of dollars in overrun costs, but the mission was finally accomplished!

Psychiatrist M. Scott Peck said, "Life is a series of problems. Do we want to moan about them or solve them?" I did try to solve those problems, but I have to admit that I moaned a lot about them, too. I don't even know if Noah could have withstood all of that! But I am grateful that we did finally succeed.

Often when dealing with tough issues, I think we feel like Charles Schultz, who said, "Sometimes I lie awake at night and ask, 'Where have I gone wrong?' Then a voice says to me, 'This is going to take more than one night.'"

I think it's important to remember that everyone has problems, no matter how high or low their station in life. We sometimes look at the lives of others, and if they are highly successful and seem to have it all together, we assume that they don't have problems. Or we believe their problems are easier to deal with than ours. That's a false belief. For example, Jeff Immelt is the CEO of General Electric, a position most leaders would greatly respect. And they might think Immelt's lofty position would protect him from problems. But Immelt said this after the September 11 attack. "My second day as chairman, a plane that I lease, flying with engines I built, crashed into a building that I insure, and it was covered with a network I own." That's a day with a lot of problems.

Don't Do This...

The key to overcoming problems and learning from them is to approach them the right way. Over the years, I've learned that problems get better or worse based on what you do or don't do when you face them. First, let me give you the don'ts:

1. Don't Underestimate the Problem

This is certainly a lesson I learned the hard way from experience. My biggest mistake in the effort to build the facility in San Diego was grossly underestimating the problem. I was naïve, and I overestimated my prior building experience. Constructing a small building in rural Indiana or small-town Ohio is nothing like navigating the bureaucracy of Southern California! It would be like a high school baseball player being asked to manage a team playing in the World Series.

Many problems go unresolved or are managed ineffectively because we do not take them seriously enough. Years ago I read a wonderful book by Robert H. Schuller entitled, *Tough Times Don't Last But Tough People Do*. The following paragraph helped me as a young leader to find a more realistic view of my problems and myself:

Never underestimate a problem or your power to cope with it. Realize that the problem you are facing has been faced by millions of human beings. You have untapped potential for dealing with a problem if you will take the problem and your own undeveloped, unchanneled powers seriously. Your reaction to a problem, as much as the problem itself, will determine the outcome. I have seen people face the most catastrophic problems with a positive mental attitude, turning their problems into creative experiences. They turned their scars into stars.[2]

When I first read that paragraph, I became inspired. It made me believe that the size of the person is more important than the size of the problem.

Our perspective on problems is so important. Shug Jordan, a former football and basketball coach at Auburn University, was reported to be explaining to one of his new coaches how to recruit ball players for the team when he asked, "Do we want the player who gets knocked down but doesn't get back up?"

"No," said the new coach, "we don't want him."

"Do we want the player who gets knocked down, gets back up, gets knocked down, gets back up, gets knocked down, gets back up?"

"Yes," said the new coach, "we want him!"

"No, we don't," said Jordan. "We want the guy who keeps knocking everyone down!" The bigger the person, the smaller the problem.

2. Don't Overestimate the Problem

Some people experience one problem three or more times. They experience it the first time when they worry about the problem. They experience it the second time when it actually occurs. And they live it again as they keep reliving it! I've done that. Have you? When faced with a problem, my first instinct is often to exaggerate its impact. Do that and you may be defeated before the problem ever occurs!

Cy Young was one of the greatest pitchers in major league baseball. After his career was over, he commented on the tendencies of managers to take their starters out of the game at the slightest hint of trouble. He observed, "In our day when a pitcher got into trouble in a game, instead of taking him out, our manager would leave him in and tell him to pitch his way out of trouble." Sometimes the problem is not as big a problem as we anticipate, and by tackling it, we shrink it down in size.

In an interview, leadership author and professor John Kotter said that one of his executive students gave him a two-page letter that his CEO had sent out. Part One said, "We're in a mess. Denial doesn't help. Here are some statistics to show it."

Part Two said, "It is useful to look at history. Thirty years ago this company was in a worse mess. Look at us now. We're ten times bigger. The U.S. economy had deeper recessions every twenty years in the nineteenth century. And here we are——the most powerful nation on earth."

Part Three said, "We've got to link arms and address this thing, and it's going to start with me. I'm going to try my damnedest to figure out (1) how this doesn't hurt us and (2) how we can find opportunities in this. Because there are opportunities."

The last part was, "Here's what I'm going to do, and here's what I need your help with." The final note was hopeful but not naïve.

It seems to me that the CEO was doing his best to neither underestimate nor overestimate the problem the company was facing, but rather to look at it realistically and tackle it.

3. Don't Wait for the Problem to Solve Itself

That brings us to the next lesson I've learned about problems. You can't wait for them to solve themselves. Patience is a virtue in problem solving if you are at the same time doing all that you can to fix the situation. It is not a virtue if you are waiting, hoping that the problem will solve itself or just go away.

Problems demand that we pay them attention. Why? Because left alone they almost always get worse. Nina DiSesa, who led the ad agency McCann Erickson in the late 1990s, observed, "When you step into a turnaround situation, you can safely assume four things: morale is low, fear is high, the good people are halfway out the door, and the slackers are hiding." Those things won't improve on their own. They require intentional problem solving and active leadership.

4. Don't Aggravate the Problem

Not only do problems not solve themselves, but we can actually make them worse by how we respond to them. One of the things I've told staff members for years is that problems are like fires, and every person carries around two buckets. One bucket has water, and the other gasoline. When you come across a problem, you can use the bucket of water to try to put the fire out. Or you can pour gasoline on it and make it explode. Same problem, two different results.

Taking a potentially volatile situation and making it worse is only one way of aggravating a problem. We can also make problems worse when we respond to them poorly. Some of the ways we can do that include:

- Losing our perspective
- Giving up important priorities and values

- Losing our sense of humor
- Feeling sorry for ourselves
- Blaming others for our situation

Instead, we need to try to remain positive. Author Norman Vincent Peale asserted, "Positive thinking is how you think about a problem. Enthusiasm is how you feel about a problem. The two together determine what you do about a problem."

> "Positive thinking is how you think about a problem. Enthusiasm is how you feel about a problem. The two together determine what you do about a problem."
> —*Norman Vincent Peale*

Do This...

If you want to overcome problems and turn them into opportunities for learning, then I recommend that you do the following:

1. Do Anticipate the Problem

They say the punch that knocks you out is not necessarily the hardest one, but the one you didn't see coming. I once read about a prisoner in Sydney, Australia, who succeeded in breaking out of jail. He hid in the underpinnings of a delivery truck that had stopped briefly in the prison warehouse. He held on desperately as the truck drove out of the prison. A few moments later, when the truck finally stopped, the prisoner dropped down to the ground and rolled outward to freedom. Unfortunately he discovered that he was now in the courtyard of another prison five miles from the first. He sure didn't see that coming.

Of course, anticipating problems doesn't mean worrying all the time about everything that *could* go wrong. I enjoy the story of a man who was awakened by his wife. She thought she heard a burglar down-stairs. He slowly got up, went grumpily downstairs, and found himself staring into the barrel of a gun. The burglar ordered him to hand over all the household valuables, then started to leave. The husband stopped him. "Before you go," he said, "I'd like you to come upstairs and meet my wife. She's been expecting you every night for over thirty years."

2. Do Communicate the Problem

Former college football head coach Lou Holtz quipped, "Don't tell your problems to people! Eighty percent don't care and the other 20 percent are glad you have them." I laugh every time I think about that statement, because for the most part it is true. On the other hand, if we work with other people, we *must* communicate about our problem to the people whom it will affect. We owe them that. Besides the solution often lies in receiving help from someone else who is able to help us solve it.

> "Don't tell your problems to people! Eighty percent don't care and the other 20 percent are glad you have them."
> —Lou Holtz

Lack of communication and poor communication not only prevent us from solving problems, they can also create problems of their own. Bernd Pischetsrieder, former chairman of Volkswagen, said, "I do know that the principal conflicts I have experienced have always had one simple cause: miscommunication. Either I didn't understand what other people wanted, or they didn't understand what I wanted. These conflicts were caused by a lack of communication and not just merely misunderstanding someone's words, but also misunderstanding a person's intentions and the background from which someone has formed an opinion."

Whenever I'm preparing to communicate regarding a problem, I first try to gather information and find out people's experiences and perspectives. That process helps me to better understand what's going on and where everyone is coming from. Sometime I find out that the problem we have isn't the problem I thought it was. Occasionally, I discover that the problem I was concerned about wasn't actually a problem at all. Or that people on the team are already solving it. But no matter what, whether it involves family, friends, employees, or teammates, when you are facing problems, it's crucial that you all get on the same page and work on it together.

3. Do Evaluate the Problem

They say you should never open a can of worms unless you plan to go fishing. Too often, I've been quick to open up the can without first thinking through the situation. I would have been better off trying to evaluate first.

> Never open a can of worms unless you plan to go fishing.

How do you do that? First, you need to ask yourself, *What is the issue?* If someone says the moon is a hundred miles from Earth, no big deal. Let it go. Unless you're a scientist, it doesn't matter. If someone is about to eat food that is poisoned, deal with it immediately. You have to adjust to the size and weight of the issue. Sometimes that's hard to do, especially for a type A person who wants to jump in on every little thing. To keep myself from doing that, for years I had a laminated card on my desk with the question, "Does this REALLY MATTER?" It helped me keep perspective when an issue was being discussed.

The second question you need to ask is, *Who is involved?* Often problems are problems because of the people in the middle of them. Some are like Charlie Brown in the classic *Peanuts* television special,

A Charlie Brown Christmas. When he just can't seem get into the Christmas spirit, Linus tells him, "You're the only person I know who can take a wonderful season like Christmas and turn it into a problem."

As you evaluate problems, try to maintain perspective, and always keep the end in mind. I saw something when I lived in southern Indiana that captures this idea concisely. It was a sign on a farm fence that said, "If you cross this field you had better do it in 9.8 seconds. The bull can do it in 10 seconds."

4. Do Appreciate the Problem

Appreciating a problem is counterintuitive for many people. Most people see a problem as a nuisance and try to avoid it. However, if we have the right attitude and appreciate a problem, not only will we work harder to solve it, but we will also learn and grow from it. Problems always bring opportunities, and opportunities always bring problems. The two go hand in hand. If we can learn to appreciate that truth, we have a real advantage in life.

A fantastic illustration of the benefits of adversity can be seen in the way an eagle meets the challenge of turbulent winds.

- *Turbulent winds cause the eagle to fly higher.* There is tremendous lifting power in the thermal updrafts of turbulent winds. These updrafts cause the eagle to reach great heights as he soars with them.
- *Turbulent winds give the eagle a larger view.* The higher the eagle flies, the larger will be his perspective of the land below him. From this higher position the sharp eyes of the eagle are able to see much more.

- *Turbulent winds lift the eagle above harassment.* At lower elevations the eagle is often harassed by suspicious crows, disgruntled hawks, and other smaller birds. As the eagle soars higher, he leaves behind all these distractions.
- *Turbulent winds allow the eagle to use less effort.* The wings of the eagle are designed for gliding in the winds. The feather structure prevents stalling, reduces the turbulence, and produces a relatively smooth ride with minimum effort—even in rough winds.
- *Turbulent winds allow the eagle to stay up longer.* The eagle uses winds to soar and glide for long periods of time. In the winds, the eagle first glides in long shallow circles downward and then spirals upward with a thermal updraft.
- *Turbulent winds help the eagle to fly faster.* Normally, the eagle flies at a speed of about 50 miles an hour. However, when he glides in wind currents, speeds of well over 100 miles per hour are not uncommon.[3]

A problem isn't really a problem unless you allow it to be a problem. A problem is really an opportunity. If you can see it that way, then every time you face a problem, you will realize that you're really faced with an opportunity. At the least, it's an opportunity to learn. But it could become even more if you pursue solving it with the right attitude.

In 1960, when John F. Kennedy was a senator campaigning for the presidency, he gave a successful speech to a crowd at the Alamo in San Antonio, Texas, site of the historic battle where a small group of American heroes was defeated by the Mexican army. When Kennedy finished, he wanted to make a quick exit, so he said to Maury

Mathers, a local politician, "Maury, let's get out of here. Where's the back door?"

"Senator," Maury replied, "if there had been a back door to the Alamo, there wouldn't have been any heroes."[4]

If you and I want to gain the full benefit from every problem, challenge, and loss, we need to stop looking for the back door and face the difficulty with the determination to gain something from it. Do that, and you can become a hero in your own life.

10

Bad Experiences: The Perspective for Learning

It would be wonderful if the gun in the airport incident were the only dumb major mistake I've made in life. Sadly, that is not the case. That was the worst of them, but there have been many other incidents of stupid-is-as-stupid-does.

A classic one occurred in 2000. At that time, I was working on my book *The 17 Indisputable Laws of Teamwork*. About a month before the manuscript was due, I was scheduled to go on a two-week speaking tour in Africa. *What a great opportunity to finish writing the book,* I thought. And it was. I can still remember the satisfaction I felt at Victoria Falls, when I finished the work. It was on the very day I was to return to the United States. With a great sense of completion and fulfillment, I put the manuscript into my briefcase and headed home.

When I arrived back in the United States, my son-in-law Steve picked me up at the Atlanta airport. He was going to drive us straight up to Highlands, North Carolina, because Margaret and our daughter Elizabeth, who is married to Steve, were waiting there for us. After the long flight, I was hungry, so we stopped to pick up some Mexican food on our way out of Atlanta, and off we went.

As Steve drove, I rode in the passenger seat and got ready to eat, but I managed to drop my fork. I tried to reach down and find it, but it was hopeless. "Steve, pull over, will you?" I finally asked. And Steve, who is used to this sort of thing from me, pulled over to the side of the road so that I could make my search. I got out, started feeling around, and still I couldn't find it. Finally, I moved my briefcase, which was sitting beside me on the floor, and there was the fork. Fantastic! I could finally eat! I climbed back in, and off we went.

Oh No!

About twenty minutes later, after I'd finished my food, I looked over and said, "Where's my briefcase?" That's when it hit me. When I was looking for the fork, I had taken out my briefcase and set it on the side of the road. *And I never put it back in the car!*

The loss of the briefcase would be bad enough, but you have to understand that when I write, I don't use a computer. I write everything out on a legal pad by hand using a four-color pen and taping quotes and illustrations right on the paper. There is no backup. There's only one copy, and that copy represents months of work.

We had gone twenty miles by the time I realized what I had done. The instant I figured it out, we turned around. And while we were driving back, I was already calling Linda, my assistant. She lived only five miles from that spot, and I knew she could get to it quickly, probably before we did.

A few minutes later my phone rang. I answered with great hope, but my heart sank when she gave me the news that the briefcase was gone! When Steve and I arrived, there was Linda. Sure enough, she was in the right place, but there was no sign of the briefcase. I felt sick.

We noticed that there were a few stores close by, so we went to each and asked if anyone had picked up a briefcase and turned it in there. No luck. The briefcase and my manuscript were gone!

Over the next several days, I was overwhelmed with emotions. I felt:

- *Stupidity:* I wondered how anyone could be smart enough to write a book and dumb enough to leave it on the side of the road.
- *Anxiety:* It was hopeless to think I'd ever see my briefcase again, so I spent hours writing down whatever I could remember from the manuscript. After a couple of days, I came to the conclusion that I could rewrite the book, but it would take at least six months. And because I was feeling so low emotionally, I felt certain that it would not be as good as the original.
- *Frustration:* It looked like there was no way to meet my publisher's deadline. I had wasted months of my time. If only I had made a copy. But I hadn't.
- *Despair:* Then I started to doubt myself. *What if I couldn't rewrite the book at all?* I wondered.

At that time, the poem "The Land of Beginning Again" by Louisa Fletcher Tarkington came to mind:

I wish that there were some wonderful place
Called the Land of Beginning Again
Where all our mistakes and all our heart-aches,

And all of our poor selfish grief
Could be dropped, like a shabby old coat, at the door,
And never put on again.[1]

While I was feeling discouraged, Linda was undaunted. She started calling local police precincts to see if the briefcase had been turned in to them. On the fourth day, Linda struck gold. The briefcase had been turned in. Better yet, everything was still in it—including the manuscript. We all rejoiced, the book was published, and all was well. However, even to this day, whenever I pick up *The 17 Indisputable Laws of Teamwork* I think of my bad experience and the lessons I learned from it.

Putting Your Losses into Perspective

Obviously, no one goes out of the way to have bad experiences. But the truth is that the negative experiences we have can do us some good, if we are willing to let them. The next time you have a bad experience, allow it to help you do the following:

1. Accept Your Humanness

No matter how hard we try, no matter how talented we are, no matter how high our standards may be, we will fail. Why? Because we're human. Nobody is perfect, and when we have bad experiences, we should allow that to be a reminder to us that we need to accept our imperfections.

I came across an article by Larry Libby written about President George H. W. Bush that reminded me that everyone has a bad day, even a president. Libby wrote,

He longed for a Single Dazzling Moment. A defining performance in a long and storied career. It was a state dinner in Tokyo. The political and economic shoguns of Japan arranged themselves around a table that shone with white silk, gold utensils, and brilliant floral arrangements. American business moguls were there, too, silently willing their leader to throw all the condescending smiles back in their hosts' faces. The world's media packed the back of the hall, microphones open, video cameras rolling. Trouble was, he'd been feeling a little funny all morning. A little light-headed. A little shaky. But this was one of those times when personal comfort had to be shunted aside. These meetings—this very dinner—carried huge implications for American business and the world economy. He simply had to be in top form. He simply had to make a commanding impression. He had just worked his way through the second course—raw salmon with caviar—and was now staring dubiously at the third—grilled beef with pepper sauce. He turned to his left and nodded at his smiling host, Prime Minister Kiichi Miyazawa. And then he threw up in the Prime Minister's lap and tumbled to the floor. As his alarmed wife, security agents, and personal physician knelt on the floor beside him, he groaned, "Roll me under the table until the dinner's over." Lying there on that fine oriental carpet, President George Bush may have been thinking about the videotape. He may have been visualizing CNN replaying the whole thing. Over and over. In prime time. In slow motion. In full color. And he would have been right.

A little later, when Press Secretary Marlin Fitzwater stood before the massed media of the Western world, he was obliged to say what ought to have been obvious to everyone.

"The President," he intoned, "is a human being. The President gets the flu like everyone else."[2]

When you have a bad experience, I hope you will give yourself some grace—whether it's a matter beyond your control or because you make a mistake. You're only human, and you shouldn't expect yourself to be perfect.

2. Learn to Laugh at Yourself and Life

I have discovered that if I'm willing see the humor in my bad experiences, I will never run out of things to laugh about. Does laughing fix everything? Maybe not. But it helps. Laughter is like changing a

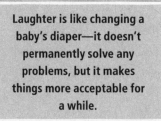

Laughter is like changing a baby's diaper—it doesn't permanently solve any problems, but it makes things more acceptable for a while.

baby's diaper—it doesn't permanently solve any problems, but it makes things more acceptable for a while.

One of my favorite stories related to bad experiences is about a man who sent a business friend flowers on the day of his grand opening. However, the order was handled badly by the florist, and the businessman received a bouquet that was intended for a funeral. It was accompanied by a card that said: "My deepest sympathy during this time of sorrow."

When the man called his friend on the phone to wish him well, his friend was confused. "Why in the world did you send me these sympathy flowers?" asked the businessman.

The man who had sent the flowers went immediately to the florist to demand an explanation.

"I am terribly sorry about the mix up with the flowers," said the florist, who was obviously upset, "but I hope you will be understanding. Your situation is not half as bad as the one down at the funeral home. The folks there received *your* flowers accompanied by the card, which said: "Best wishes in your new location.""

President Abraham Lincoln, who led the United States through its darkest hour, was well known for finding ways to laugh at himself and the difficult situations he faced. In fact, he was criticized for it. But that didn't stop him. Addressing a group of critics, he said, "Gentlemen, why don't you laugh? With the fearful strain that is upon me night and day, if I did not laugh, I should die."

Sometimes it's hard to see the humor during a difficult experience. Often I say to myself, "This is not funny today, but tomorrow it may be." That was the case when I took the gun into the airport. That day, I was embarrassed and humiliated. But only a few days later, I was able to see the humor and absurdity of my actions. How much lighter would your load be if you were to find ways to laugh when you were faced with bad experiences?

3. Keep the Right Perspective

When you have a bad experience, which of the following phrases is most likely to represent your thinking?

- I never wanted to do that task to start with, so who cares?
- I'm a failure and my life is over.
- I want to give up and never try again.
- I'm gaining experience from my mistakes; I wonder if I can get some help.
- I now know three ways that won't work, so I'll try again.

Your answer says more about your perspective than it does about the bad experience. That's why the responses to the same bad experience can be so varied.

Author and speaker Denis Waitley says, "Mistakes are painful when they happen, but years later a collection of mistakes is what is called experience." Seeing difficulties as experience is a matter of perspective. It's like the difference between going in the ocean as a small child and as an adult. When you're little, the waves look massive, and you fear that they may overwhelm you. As an adult, the same size waves may be seen as a source of relaxation and fun.

> "Mistakes are painful when they happen, but years later a collection of mistakes is what is called experience."
> —Denis Waitley

When facing difficulties, maintaining perspective isn't always easy, but it is worth fighting for. As you work to maintain the right point of view, try to keep these three things in mind.

Don't Base Your Self-Worth on a Bad Experience

You are not your performance. And you don't have to be defined by your worst moments. So don't base your self-image on those things. Instead, try to understand and accept your value as a human being. If you fail, don't ever tell yourself, "I am a failure." Instead, keep things in perspective and say, "I may have missed that one, but I'm still okay. I can still be a winner!"

Don't Feel Sorry for Yourself

One of the worst things you can do to lose perspective is to start feeling sorry for yourself. Okay, if you have a bad experience, you can feel sorry for yourself for twenty-four hours, but then after that, pick yourself up and get moving again. Because if you start to wallow, you just might get stuck.

Psychiatrist Frederic Flach in his book *Resilience* points out that survivors of bad experiences don't let the negatives in their lives define them, and they don't wallow in self-pity. They don't believe their negative experience is the worst thing in the world. Instead, they think, *What happened to me may have been bad, but other people are worse off. I'm not giving in.*

If you find yourself in the aftermath of a bad experience, try to remember that if you're still breathing, it could have been worse. Try to focus on the good you can make of the difficulty. Because of the experience you've gained, you may even be able to help others who have gone through similar difficulties.

Do Consider Your Failures as a Process to Learn and Improve

When we fail or have a bad experience, we need to learn to become more like scientists and inventors. When their work fails, they call it an experiment that didn't work. Or they say they tested a hypothesis. Or they term it data collection. They keep their perspective, avoid taking it personally, learn from it, and leverage it for future success. What a great way to look at things.

Psychologist Dr. Joyce Brothers asserted, "The person interested in success has to learn to view failure as a healthy, inevitable part of the process of getting to the top." Or to put it another way, as longtime baseball manager Casey Stengel did: "You gotta lose'm sometimes. When you do, lose'm right."

> "You gotta lose'm sometimes. When you do, lose'm right."
> —Casey Stengel

4. Don't Give Up

Swimmer Eric Shanteau has called the 2004 U.S. Olympic Swim Trials "the most devastating experience of my life." That's quite a statement considering Shanteau was diagnosed with cancer in 2008. What would make those Olympic trails such a difficult experience? He finished third—and only the first two places in the trials make the Olympic team. In fact, it happened twice during those trials. He missed second place in the 400-meter individual medley by 0.99 seconds and the 200-meter individual medley by 0.34 seconds. Shanteau recalls,

> The initial reaction was anger. I remember walking down that deck being very frustrated. You see a lifelong goal slip out of your fingers in the last five meters and it's brutal. It was very, very hard. I didn't want anything to do with the sport for about seven weeks after. Finishing third at the trials, you might as well get last.[3]

He may have wanted to give up, but he didn't. He got back in the pool and trained for another four years. His reward in 2008 was making the team in the 200-meter breaststroke. Though he didn't medal in Beijing, he did swim a personal best. He kept training and returned to the Olympics again in 2012 in London. He won a gold medal by swimming the breaststroke for the team in the 4×100-meter medley relay.

What does Shanteau know about bad experiences that most people don't? He knows that:

- Failure is the cost of seeking new challenges.
- Ninety percent of those who fail are not actually defeated; they simply quit.

- There are two kinds of people in regards to setbacks: splatters, who hit the bottom, fall apart, and stay on the bottom; and bouncers, who hit rock bottom, pull themselves together, and bounce back up.
- Success lies in having made the effort; failure lies in never having tried.
- Most failures are people who have the habit of making excuses.

If you want to succeed in life, you can't give up.

Author and speaker Og Mandino, whose work influenced me greatly, said, "Whenever you make a mistake or get knocked down by life, don't look back at it too long. Mistakes are life's way of teaching you. Your capacity for occasional blunders is inseparable from your capacity to reach your goals. No one wins them all, and your failures, when they happen, are just part of your growth. Shake off your blunders. How will you know your limits without an occasional failure?" He goes on to say, "Your turn will come." What great advice!

5. Don't Let Your Bad Experience Become Worse Experiences

Back in the days when the only way to watch sports was on network television (unless you actually went to the event), the premier show was *ABC's Wide World of Sports*. For three and a half decades, the show opened with various sports images and a narrator saying, "Spanning the globe to bring you the constant variety of sports...the thrill of victory...the agony of defeat." To illustrate the latter, it always showed a ski jumper heading down ramp, and then suddenly going off course, spinning, crashing through the supporting structure, and then bouncing on the ground. It looked like a horrendous crash.

What most people didn't know was that the skier's fall wasn't a freak accident. He *chose* to fall rather than to finish the jump. An experienced jumper, he realized that the ramp had become icy, and he was picking up so much speed that if he completed the jump, he would probably land far beyond the sloped landing area and hit level ground, which might have killed him. So instead, he changed directions. What looked like a catastrophically painful accident actually resulted in no more than a headache, whereas what would have looked like a great jump might have been fatal.

The lesson to be learned from this is that one of the things that's worse than a bad experience is letting that bad experience become an even worse one—if you have the power to stop it. How do you gain the power to recognize when an experience is going from bad to worse? By learning from previous experiences using critical thinking skills.

If you find yourself in a bad experience, one of the first things you should try to do is determine if the bad experience is a result of ignorance or stupidity. Ignorance means that you didn't have the necessary knowledge to do the right thing. A person can hardly be blamed for that. Stupidity is the result of knowing what to do but not acting upon that knowledge.

BAD EXPERIENCES BASED ON IGNORANCE	BAD EXPERIENCES BASED ON STUPIDITY
"I didn't know better, so I did it."	"I knew better, but I did it anyway."
"I didn't know better, so I didn't do it."	"I knew better, yet I didn't do it."

Bad experiences based on ignorance require learning. If you have a teachable spirit, as I discussed in chapter 7, not only can you stop a bad experience from getting worse, you can make it better. On the other hand, bad experiences based on stupidity usually come from lack of discipline and poor choices. Changing those requires not only teachability but also a change in behavior. If you don't make those changes, the bad experiences will likely keep coming and keep getting worse.

6. Let the Bad Experience Lead You to a Good Experience

Everyone can relate to having bad experiences in life. But not everyone works to turn the bad experiences into good ones. That is possible only when we turn our losses into learning experiences. You just have to remember that bad experiences are bad only if we fail to learn from them. And good experiences are almost always a result of previous bad experiences.

For years I have been a pen collector. Maybe that's because I actually use a pen, not a computer, when I write. In my search for interesting pens, I came across an interesting story about a young insurance agent who had been working to win a new client for quite a long time. Finally, he was successful and persuaded the man to take out a large policy.

The agent arrived at the potential client's office with the contract ready for a signature. He placed it on the man's desk and took out a fountain pen. But as he removed the pen's cap, it leaked ink all over the contract, ruining it.

The agent prepared another contract a quickly as he could, but by the time he returned, the window of opportunity was closed. The would-be client had changed his mind and declined to give the agent his business.

The young agent was so disgusted with the pen and the problem it had caused that he devoted his time to the development of a reliable fountain pen. That young agent was Lewis E. Waterman, and his company has been in the business of producing fine pens for 120 years. He not only took a bad experience and turned it into a good experience, but he created a well-respected and lucrative business from it.

I started this chapter with the story of my bad experience losing my briefcase and the manuscript inside it. How did I take that bad experience and turn it into a better one? I decided that day to always make a copy of anything I write in addition to the one in my possession. I also learned to get anything I create into the hands of Linda, my assistant, as soon as I am done with it, whether it's a chapter of a book or a lecture I've written. And I *never* carry a complete manuscript in my briefcase.

Will I lose my writing material in the future? Probably. I am just not very careful. Will it be the only copy of my material when I lose it? Never! That's the perspective I've gained from that bad experience.

His Bad Experience Was His Springboard

As you face bad experiences, it's important for you to remember that you can rarely see the benefits while you're in the midst of trouble. You usually gain perspective on the other side of it. That was certainly the case for Giuseppe, who was named for his father, an immigrant from Italy who had settled in California. Because they lived in America, the family called him Joe. But his father had his own nickname for him: Good-for-Nothing. Why did the elder Giuseppe call him that? Because Joe hated fishing. That was seen as a terrible thing by the father, because he was a fisherman. He loved the fishing business. So did all of his sons—except for Good-for-Nothing Joe. The boy didn't like being on the boat, and the smell of fish made him sick.

The boy offered to work in the office or to repair nets, but his father was simply disgusted with him and said he was good for nothing.

The boy, who was not afraid of hard work, delivered newspapers and shined shoes, giving the money to the family, but since it wasn't fishing, the elder Giuseppe saw no value in it.

Young Joe hated fishing, but he loved baseball. His older brother used to play sandlot ball, and Joe used to follow him there. And he was good—something of a legend among his playmates. When Joe was sixteen, he decided to drop out of school to become a baseball player. By the time he was through with baseball, he was a legend. He was christened as Giuseppe, but the nation came to know him as Joe DiMaggio, called the most complete player of his generation.

And his father, the elder Giuseppe, what did he think about it? Though he had wanted all of his sons to enter the family business, he was finally proud of his son and respected his accomplishments. How could he not? Joe took the bad experiences and turned them into great experiences through the perspective of learning.

11

Change: The Price of Learning

If you grew up anytime between 1950 and 1990, you probably remember Polaroid cameras. In today's era of digital photography, it may be hard for some people to understand what a big deal instant photographs were, but in their time they were revolutionary. To give you some perspective, in the early days of photographic history during the 1800s, only people with expensive cameras, darkrooms, a host of chemicals, and specific technical skills could produce photographs.

Then in 1888, Kodak developed innovations in cameras and film that put photography in nearly everyone's reach. "You press the button, we do the rest" was their slogan. The good news was anybody could be a photographer; the bad news was that he had to mail off his camera with the exposed film to a plant to be processed, and then wait days or weeks to receive his photographs. Even well into the twentieth century, when film was created that anyone could load and remove from a camera himself, seeing the photographs you shot was an exercise in patience.

Innovation Comes from Change

Edwin Land changed all that. Land, the son of a scrap-metal dealer, was born in 1909. As a boy, he became fascinated with the physics of light after reading Robert W. Wood's *Physical Optics*, one of the few books in his house. He was accepted at Harvard and attended there briefly, but dropped out to do experiments in a homemade lab he created in his New York City apartment.

Land was awarded his first patent in 1929 after he developed a process for polarization that could be used commercially. That early work eventually led to glare-reducing sunglasses, pilots' goggles for the military, filtering systems for photography, and the first 3-D movie system. Land started his company in 1937, with the help of an investor. In 1940, it was named the Polaroid Corporation. During World War II, the company made a fortune. But Land was best known for what has been called his ability to "invent on demand." An Air Force general once called Land asking advice for a problem with gun sights. One of Land's colleagues recounted, "Land's reply was that he would fly down to Washington the next day to describe the solution. The general said, 'Oh, so you have a solution?' And Land responded, 'No, but I'll have one by then.' And he did."[1]

That ability to innovate is said to have given birth to the idea of instant photography. One day in 1943 while on vacation, Land was taking pictures of his daughter, and she asked him, "Why can't I see the picture now?"[2] With Land's genius for problem solving and invention, the mental gears started turning. He started figuring out how to create a camera and film that could produce a paper photograph on the spot. Christopher Bonanos, author of *Instant: The Story of Polaroid*, writes, "Everything he'd learned in his previous work—about filters, about making tiny crystals and thin films, about optics, even about manufacturing and outsourcing—came into play."[3] Land later said that he was able to rough out the details of the system in a few hours, "except," he said, "for the ones that took from 1943 to 1972 to solve."[4]

The Land camera by Polaroid was first sold to the public in November 1948. It produced a sepia-toned photograph in about sixty seconds. At the time, it was an astounding technological innovation. The questions was, would anyone buy it? Land's colleagues believed he was too optimistic when he hoped to sell 50,000 cameras per year. But Land was right. People loved it. At its debut, their entire stock of cameras sold out within hours. By 1953, Polaroid had sold 900,000 units.[5]

During the next two decades, Polaroid continued to change and innovate. They retired the sepia film and developed a fine black-and-white, which they said was the toughest single task the company ever faced. They recruited legendary photographer Ansel Adams as a consultant and camera user. Whenever they faced technical problems, such as photographs that faded, they solved it. And they developed a way to create instant photographs in color. They learned from their mistakes and kept getting better.

Polaroid was founded on change. They spent extraordinary amounts of money on research and development, creating new products and processes. And their early cameras displayed elegant designs, often the work of industrial artists. They kept innovating. In the 1970s, photographers were shooting a *billion* Polaroid photographs each year.[6]

The End of Innovation

In the mid-1970s, Polaroid fought against Kodak, who introduced an instant camera that Land believed infringed on Polaroid's patents. The battle lasted over fourteen years and wasn't settled until 1990. But by that time, Land had retired (in 1980). And Polaroid was in deep trouble. People were no longer buying their products. Bonanos writes:

> Ask Polaroid people where things started to go wrong—was it at some point in the 1980s? earlier? later?—and everyone has a different answer. One blames inflexible engineers, another financial missteps.... What's clear, though, is that the decline began almost imperceptibly. In 1978, Polaroid had more than 20,000 employees.... By 1991 ... 5,000.... A decade later, even having received that immense windfall [nearly $1 billion from the Kodak settlement], Polaroid was bankrupt.[7]

In fact, between 2001 and 2009 Polaroid declared bankruptcy twice and was sold three times.

What happened? The company that had been founded on innovation and thrived on change stopped paying the price of learning. Where its best thinkers had spent their time creating innovative solutions to problems and introducing revolutionary products that the public didn't know it wanted—but loved—the new emphasis was on rehashing old products with minor cosmetic updates. The company under Edwin Land had put its best resources into research and development while outsourcing manufacturing, but it then shifted its focus to manufacturing and cutting costs. The days of innovation and change were over—and at a time when photography was experiencing its most rapid change.

Ironically, Polaroid had a shot at introducing an early digital camera. The idea was that the leader in instant photography would become the leader in instant imaging, but they abandoned the project because it didn't include their regular revenue stream of film sales.[8] They also were in a position to pioneer inkjet technology. But when upper management decided that the quality of the technology "would never be photographic," they killed the project.

Had Land still been leading the company, he probably would have continued to fight for a solution, paying the price to *invent* a way to make the quality high enough. That's what he had always done in the past. Instead, under new leadership, Polaroid slowly faded away to nothing. That's what happens when people won't pay the price of learning by being willing to change.

Why People Resist Change

Change is not embraced by most people. I used to think leaders loved change and everyone else didn't. Now after decades of teaching and investing in leaders, I have come to realize that leaders resist change as much as followers do—unless the change is their idea! The truth is that just about everybody resists change. Why? Because...

Change Can Feel Like a Personal Loss

Pioneering radio host George V. Denny Jr. once told the story of a New York City newspaper reporter who was sent to Maine to interview an old man who was nearing his hundredth birthday. The reporter approached the gentleman politely and said, "Sir, you must have see a great many changes during your hundred years."

The old man looked at the reporter intently. "Yes," he replied, "and I've been against all of 'em!"

Novelist Andre Gide observed, "One doesn't discover new lands without consenting to lose sight of the shore for a very long time." That loss can be very frightening, and it can sometimes feel like a personal loss. It makes you wonder if the elderly man from Maine felt like the

> "One doesn't discover new lands without consenting to lose sight of the shore for a very long time."
> —Andre Gide

changes he continually experienced were a personal affront! But the truth of the matter is that though change *feels* personal, it isn't. The world keeps changing and it affects everyone, whether they like it or not.

Poet and philosopher Ralph Waldo Emerson had an insightful take on this. He asserted, "For every thing we gain we lose something." We like gaining, but we don't like losing. We want to have the one without the other. But life doesn't work that way. Every beginning ends something. Every ending begins something new. We are continually making trades in life. Unfortunately, if you resist change, you are trading your potential to grow for your comfort. No change means no growth.

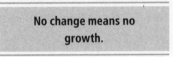

No change means no growth.

Change Feels Awkward

Change always feels different. Because it's unfamiliar, it often doesn't feel right. Let me give you an example. Take a moment right now and clasp your hands together with your fingers interlaced. That probably feels very comfortable. Why? Because you naturally place your hands a certain way, with one thumb over the other. Now clasp your hands the opposite way by trading the position of your thumbs and moving your fingers over just one finger. How does that feel? It's probably uncomfortable. You never clasp your hands that way.

Is it wrong to clasp your hands this other way? No. Is it an inferior way of clasping hands? No. It's just different. And different feels awkward. But you *can* get used to it. Don't believe me? Every day for the next two weeks, clasp your hands the opposite way from what you're used to. By the end of that time, it will feel almost as comfortable as your natural way.

I experienced this awkwardness as a golfer because I taught myself how to play. Since I'd had no instruction, I was worried that I had developed a lot of bad habits. When I did finally talk to a professional golfer to get some lessons, he said, "You've got only one problem." I was relieved for a moment. Then he told me what it was: "You're too close to the golf ball after you hit it!"

Becoming better meant I would have to change everything: my grip, my stance, my posture, my swing. Every bit of it felt awkward. And what was really demoralizing was that I didn't see immediate improvement. There were times when under pressure I would resort to my old swing. I knew it was wrong, but it brought me security. I wanted the bad that I knew instead of the good I hadn't mastered. I had to overcome that awkwardness to improve my game, and after years of struggle I finally did.

Change Goes against Tradition

When I received my first leadership position in an organization, I can't tell you how many times I heard the phrase "We've never done it that way before." It seemed like every time I wanted to make an improvement, I heard someone extol the virtues of resisting change. I can't tell you how frustrating that was, especially when the person who said it couldn't tell me *why* it had always been done the way it had been done.

A Duke of Cambridge was quoted as saying, "Any change at any time is to be deplored." Why would he profess something like that? Probably because he valued tradition. And there's nothing wrong with tradition, as long as a person doesn't become a slave to it. The person who insists on using yesterday's methods in today's world won't be in business tomorrow.

Some people believe that nothing should ever be done until everyone is convinced that it ought to be done. The problem with that is it takes so long to convince them that by the time they finally agree to the change, it's time to move on to something else. No wonder some people believe that progress means moving backward slowly. They bring life to the old riddle: How many traditionalists does it take to change a lightbulb? Answer: Four. One to put in the new bulb and three tell you how wonderful the old bulb was.

> The person who insists on using yesterday's methods in today's world won't be in business tomorrow.

How People Respond to Change

Because people don't like change, most of them don't react to it very well. And their response creates more problems for them. Here's what I mean:

Most People Change Only Enough to Get Away from Problems, Not Enough to Fix Them

For many years I've counseled and mentored people, and I have come to the conclusion that many people are like Lucy in the comic strip *Peanuts*. In one installment, Lucy says, "Boy, do I feel crabby."

Her younger brother Linus responds, "Maybe I can be of help. Why don't you just take my place here in front of the TV while I go and fix you a nice snack? Sometimes we all need a little pampering to help us feel better."

Linus returns with a sandwich, chocolate chip cookies, and a glass of milk. He says, "Now, is there anything else I can get you? Is there anything I haven't thought of?"

"Yes, there's one thing you haven't thought of," Lucy replies, taking the tray. "I don't wanna feel better!"

Most people would rather change their circumstances to improve their lives when instead they need to change themselves to improve their circumstances. They put in just enough effort to distance themselves from their problems without ever trying to go after the root, which can often be found in themselves. Because they don't try to change the source of their problems, their problems keep coming back at them.

> Most people would rather change their circumstances to improve their lives when instead they need to change themselves to improve their circumstances.

Positive change and a willingness to learn are personal responsibilities. I agree with my friend Julio Melara, who says: "If your career, marriage, job, and life are to improve, you must change. In the mirror you are looking at the problem and the solution. It begins with you making a decision. The people who reach their potential no matter what their background or profession think in terms of improvement." If you want to get better, you need to be willing to change.

Most People Do the Same Thing the Same Way, Yet Expect Different Results

A letter was returned to the Post Office. Marked on the envelope were the words, "He's dead." Through an oversight the letter was again sent to the same address. It was again returned, with the following note: "He's still dead." Too often we are like the postal worker, resending that letter yet hoping for different results.

Whenever we try something and it fails, why do we keep trying the exact same thing expecting to get different results? It doesn't make sense. What do we expect to change? Our luck? The laws of physics? How can our lives get better if we don't change? How can we become better if we don't expose ourselves to growing situations and people?

Our lives are like a trip we plan to a distant city. We set a destination, map out our route, and start driving. But we should know there will be detours and obstacles ahead. Do we ignore those and pretend they don't exist? How successful will we be if we think, *The obstacles and conditions need to adjust to me because I'm not changing*? Not very. We need to be willing to make adjustments.

Many of life's greatest discoveries are found when we're willing to go off the main road, by trying things we've never tried before. Brian Tracy in his audiobook *The Psychology of Achievement* tells the story of four men who became highly successful by age thirty-five. On average, each was involved in seventeen ventures before finding the business that made it. If they had started the first business and said, "I'm not quitting this business no matter what," they would have gotten stuck. Tenacity is a fantastic quality. But tenacity without a willingness to change and make necessary adjustments becomes dogmatism and leads to dead ends.

Entrepreneur Alan Cohen said, "To grow, you must be willing to let your present and future be totally unlike your past. Your history is not your destiny." That mind-set shows a flexibility of mind and a willingness to change, which are the price of learning.

> "To grow, you must be willing to let your present and future be totally unlike your past. Your history is not your destiny."
> —Alan Cohen

Most People See Change as a Hurtful Necessity Instead of a Helpful Opportunity

Let's face the fact: change is messy. Management expert Peter Drucker observed, "As every executive has learned, nothing new is easy. It always gets into trouble." That difficulty and sense of trouble holds a lot of people back from changing. But life is change. Being born was painful. Learning to eat was messy. Learning to walk was difficult and painful. In fact, most of the things you needed to learn in order to live were tough on you. But you didn't know any better, and you did what you needed to do to learn and grow. Now that you're an adult, you have a choice. Do you want to avoid the potential pain or endure it and pursue the opportunity?

Leadership expert Max De Pree uses the phrase "the gift of change." What a great way to look at it. Unfortunately, most people don't see change as a gift. But it is. Every time you embrace change, there is an opportunity for you to go in a positive direction, make improvements to yourself, abandon old negative habits and ways of thinking. Change allows you to examine your assumptions, rethink your strategies, and build your relationships. Without change there is no innovation, creativity, or improvement. If you are willing and able to initiate change, you will have a better opportunity to manage the change that is inevitable to everyone in life.

Most People Won't Pay the Immediate Price to Change and End Up Paying the Ultimate Price for Not Changing

My dad often said to me when I was faced with a decision that required discipline, "John, pay now so you can play later." That lesson was a constant theme in my life when I was growing up. Why? Because I always wanted to play! It was in my nature. But father kept telling me, "You can play now and pay later, or you can pay now and play later. But make no mistake: you will pay. And the longer you wait, the more you will pay, because delayed payment demands interest."

Change always requires something of us. We must pay a price for it. In fact, ongoing change and improvement require continual payment. But the process begins with the *first* payment. That first payment starts the growth process. If that first price remains unpaid, there is no growth or learning. And what will that cost you in the end? You lose potential and gain regret.

As I grow older, I have come to realize that most of our regrets will not be a result of what we did. They will come because of what we could and should have done but didn't do. The final price we pay is called missed opportunity, and that is a heavy cost.

Most People Change Only When Prompted by One of Three Things

In the end, because people are so resistant to it, change occurs only under certain conditions. In my experience, people change when:

- They *hurt* enough that they *have* to
- They *learn* enough that they *want* to
- They *receive* enough that they are *able* to

Unless one of those things happens, people don't change. Sometimes people require all three to happen before they are willing to change.

Several years ago, my publisher suggested that I start using social media to connect with people. I don't have a technical bone in my body, so the idea simply did not resonate with me. But they were persistent, and eventually I started to talk about it with my team. But honestly, I still didn't get it.

Then one night I was having dinner with my friend Norwood Davis, who has worked for my company as CFO, and I mentioned Twitter to him and how I couldn't understand any use for it.

"Let me show you," Norwood said as he pulled out his phone. As I ate my steak, Norwood tweeted that he was having dinner with me. In a matter of minutes, Norwood received dozens of replies and direct messages from people encouraging him or asking him to give me messages. And I finally understood. Twitter was a way to connect with people and communicate with them almost instantaneously.

I had finally learned enough that I wanted to change. But because I'm not technical, I still needed to receive enough to be able to change. I got that with the help of Stephanie Wetzel. She created my Twitter account, got me on Facebook, and launched my blog. Now I'm able to add value to more than half a million people at any time, any day of the week. And think about this: I'm over sixty-five and nontechnical, and yet I've still been able to enter the electronic media age. That's proof that *anybody* can change if he really wants to.

Change Is Rarely Instantaneous

As I write this chapter, I am in Johannesburg, South Africa. Just a few minutes ago, my friend Collin Sewell, who owns some Ford dealerships in Texas, texted me the following, based on a quote by Mark Batterson: "You and I are only one defining decision away from a totally different life." I believe that defining decision is the willingness to change.

> "You are only one defining decision away from a totally different life."
> —Mark Batterson

The decision to change—and keep changing—is more than simply an act of will. It is a process, one that must first be started and then managed. The process and the progress will not go at the same rate for everyone. But there are certain similarities in the process for everyone, and it usually follows this pattern:

- *New information is accepted.* The process generally doesn't begin until some kind of information is learned and accepted. This changes people's perspective so that they experience a new way of seeing things.
- A *new attitude is adopted.* When a person's perspective is challenged and then changed, there is almost always an emotional reaction. This is a critical time. If the person's attitude is good, the person can move to the next phase. If not, he or she may struggle to get over the hump.
- *New behavior is practiced.* When people believe something and feel good about it, they start to behave differently. They begin to make different choices, take action, and develop new habits.
- *New convictions influence others.* When people change, they develop new convictions. When the people changing are leaders, they influence others through their investment and ownership in their new vision.

As a leader, I find this final stage in the process most exciting, because it can be the start of wonderful things on a team or in an organization. It can set new direction, change culture, and build momentum. If you are a leader, you will probably enjoy it, too. But it's important for you to understand that not all people take ownership of change to the level where they are willing and able to be vision carriers and communicators. But the more who do, the sooner and steadier the change will occur.

Making the Changes That Count

If you want to maximize your ability to pay the price of learning and set yourself up to change, improve, and grow, then you need to do the five following things:

1. Change Yourself

Back when I used to do a lot of marriage counseling for couples, I found that most people came into the process intent on seeing the other person change. I believe that is part of the human condition: to look for the faults in others and minimize our own. But that's not how you improve any relationship.

My friend Tony Evans writes,

If you want a better world,
Composed of better nations,
Inhabited by better states,
Filled with better counties,
Made up of better cities,
Comprised of better neighborhoods,
Illuminated by better churches,
Populated by better families,
Then you'll have to start by becoming
A better person.

If you want to see positive change in your marriage, quit looking for a better person and become a better person. If you want to see positive change in your career, quit looking for a better employer and become a better employee. In life, if you want more, you must become more.

If changing yourself seems overwhelming, then start small. Howard Markman, a professor of psychology at the University of Denver, says, "Most couples in trouble think that for things to improve, extraordinary changes, if not a miracle, have to take place." That's not true. "The breakthrough," says Markman, "comes when we realize that by making even small changes in ourselves, we can effect big, positive changes." That principle is also true for individuals wanting to make changes. So if you want to make big changes, start with small ones.

2. Change Your Attitude

Many years ago, I read a quote by poet and scholar Samuel Johnson that has been a foundation of my attitude and development. Johnson asserted, "He who has so little knowledge of human nature, as to seek happiness by changing any thing but his own dispositions, will waste his life in fruitless efforts, and multiply the griefs which he purposes to remove."

Trying to change others is an exercise in futility. No one can change another person. I didn't always know this. For many years my life was filled with disappointments over other people's unwillingness to grow. For years I waited for them, hoping for progress. Too many times I have hoped circumstances would change, only to be disappointed. Anything you try to change that is outside of your control will ultimately disappoint you. What's worse, I have also discovered that when I try to change those things that are outside of my control, I start to lose control of those things within me that I can change because my focus is wrong. That's a trap to be avoided.

What's the solution? Changing my attitude. That is completely within my control, and the beauty of it is that this one change can be a major factor in changing my life for the positive. In controlling my own attitude and choosing to think correctly, I can minimize the negative effects of those around me who have bad attitudes. I can stop taking it personally when someone in my life won't change. I can see opportunities where once I saw obstacles. And the best news is that, as author and speaker Wayne Dyer says, "when you change the way you look at things, the things you look at actually begin to change."

3. Change Your Nongrowing Friends

All my life I have loved people and valued relationships. Yet early in my life I realized that most of my friends were not on the same journey I was choosing to take. After I discovered the impact that personal growth could have on a person's life, I became highly intentional about growing. Many of my friends were not. When I saw this, I realized I was going to have to choose between my future and my friends. It was a painful choice, but I chose my future.

My mother used to tell me all the time, "Birds of a feather flock together." She said this because she wanted me to be aware of any negative influences in my life when I was a boy. But the truth is just as important when applied to positive influences. If you want to be a growing person, you need to spend time with growing people. If you want to be someone who embraces positive change, you need to hang around with positive learners.

There's an old saying: "A mirror reflects a man's face, but what he is really like is shown by the kind of friends he chooses." Your friends will either stretch your vision or choke your dreams. Some will inspire you to higher heights. Others will want you to join them on the couch of life where they do their least. Because not everyone wants to see you succeed, you have to make a choice. Are you going let the people who aren't growing bring you down? Or are you going to move on? This can be a painful and difficult choice, but it can change your life for the better.

I have to admit that I'm very passionate about this, because I know how critical it is to a person's success. Think about the negative impact that can occur when you spend time with the wrong people:

- What kind of counsel do you receive when you seek it from unproductive people?
- What happens when you discuss your problems with someone incapable of contributing to the solution?
- What happens when you follow someone who isn't going anywhere?
- Where do you end up when you ask directions from someone who is lost?

There are many roads in life that lead to nowhere. And there are plenty of people who will invite you to follow them there. Wise is the person who fortifies his life with the right friendships. Every minute you spend with the wrong people takes away the time you have to spend with the right ones. Change accordingly.

> Every minute you spend with the wrong people takes away the time you have to spend with the right ones.

4. Determine to Live Differently than Average People

One of life's important questions is "Who am I?" But even more important is "Who am I becoming?" To answer that question satisfactorily, we must keep one eye on where we are and the other eye on where we will be. Most people don't do that. They have one eye on where they have been and one eye on where they are now. That tells them who they are. (Some people don't even examine themselves *that* much.) However, to know who you are becoming requires you not only to know where you are now but also to know where you're going and how you need to change to get there.

> One of life's important questions is "Who am I?" But even more important is "Who am I becoming?"

If you are determined to change and to live a life above and beyond average, know that you need to do things differently as you look ahead. You must...

Think Differently

Successful people are realistic about their problems and find positive ways to approach time. They know that hope isn't a strategy.

Handle Feelings Differently

Successful people don't allow their feelings to determine their behavior. They behave their way into feeling so that they can do what they must to grow and keep moving forward.

Act Differently

Successful people do two things that many other people don't: they initiate action, and they finish what they start. As a result, they form the habit of doing things that unsuccessful people don't.

You've probably heard the statement "If you want something you've never had, you must to do something you've never done." It's also true that if you want to become someone you have never been, you must do things you have never done. That means changing what you do every day. The secret to success can be found in your daily agenda. Average people don't put in the extra work every day to keep growing and changing.

5. Unlearn What You Know to Learn What You Don't Know

Professional baseball pitcher Satchel Paige said, "It's not what you don't know that hurts you—it's what you do know that just ain't so." That is so true. There are many things that each of us learns are wrong, and we must unlearn them if we want to get better. Unlearning them can be difficult, but that is just another price we must pay if we want to grow.

Recently I read an article by leadership coach Lance Secretan in which he describes working with intermediate skiers and in one day teaching them to do advanced skiing on moguls (bumps) and double black diamond runs (expert only). He says being able to do that so quickly confounds many skiing experts. But Secretan says the secret lies less in helping skiers learn new skills and more in helping them *unlearn* some. He writes,

> When you are frightened, you calcify your attitudes and beliefs—you resort to the familiar and close your mind. New learning is impossible, and effectiveness is impaired. An intermediate skier, facing a 60-degree pitch, will resort to old habits—a *snowplow* (the skis are wedged to slow speed) or *side slipping* (the skis are angled at 90 degrees to the incline of the slope). Until these old habits are set aside, no learning progress can be made.
>
> *Unlearning is a prerequisite for growth.* Unlearning is like seeing the world with new eyes. To unlearn, you: 1) admit that

an old practice, belief, or attitude is not solving the current problem and that doing more of it won't lead to desired outcomes; 2) open your mind—yield to the view that there are alternatives to the way you've always done it until now; 3) switch from *trying to rationalize the use of your long-favored solution* to *asking questions about how you can change, learn, and grow*; 4) commit to terminating the old way forever; and 5) practice and perfect the new way.[9]

Unlearning outdated or wrong ways of doing things can be difficult. We tend to lean on what we know, even if it's not the best for us. The secret is to allow yourself to be wrong and to be willing to change for the better. Psychiatrist David Burns says it this way: "Never give up your right to be wrong, because then you will lose the ability to learn new things and move forward with your life."

> "Never give up your right to be wrong, because then you will lose the ability to learn new things and move forward with your life."
> —David Burns

Change is difficult for all of us, yet it is essential if we want to turn our losses into gains. It is the price we must pay for learning. And don't let anyone tell you, "You can't teach an old dog new tricks." A lot of dog trainers have proven that statement to be false. Besides, the ideas in this chapter are not written for old dogs and they are not about tricks. They are for people like you and me who want to change, learn, and grow. And we can do it—if we're willing to pay the price.

12

Maturity: The Value of Learning

What do you get if you follow through with all the ideas I've been discussing in this book? Is there a pot of gold at the end of this rainbow? What happens if you:

- Cultivate Humility: The Spirit of Learning
- Face Reality: The Foundation of Learning
- Accept Responsibility: The First Step of Learning
- Seek Improvement: The Focus of Learning
- Nurture Hope: The Motivation of Learning
- Develop Teachability: The Pathway of Learning
- Overcome Adversity: The Catalyst for Learning
- Leverage Problems: The Opportunities for Learning
- Endure Bad Experiences: The Perspective for Learning, and
- Embrace Change: The Price of Learning

What happens? You are rewarded with Maturity: The Value of Learning!

When I say *maturity*, I don't mean age. Many people think maturity is a natural result of getting older. When they encounter an immature person, they say, "Give him a few years and he'll mature." Not necessarily. Maturity doesn't always accompany age. Sometimes age comes alone! No, to me a mature person is someone who has learned from losses, has gained wisdom, and possesses a strong emotional and mental stability in the face of life's difficulties.

Author William Saroyan observed, "Good people are good because they've come to wisdom through failure. We get very little wisdom from success, you know." What Saroyan is describing is this kind of maturity. To some that quality comes at an early age. For others, it never comes.

> "Good people are good because they've come to wisdom through failure. We get very little wisdom from success."
> —William Saroyan

George Reedy, who was President Lyndon Johnson's press secretary, convinced the president that he should not have any assistants who were younger than forty and who had never suffered any major disappointments in life. Why? Reedy believed they lacked the maturity needed to advise the president. People who haven't overcome major losses are prone to think they are invincible. They start to believe they are better than they really are and are inclined to misuse their power. Everyone who makes a major contribution to life knows what it is to have failures.

Fred Smith, a mentor of mine for many years, used to tell me, "I don't think God is as interested in our success as He is in our maturity." That is a sobering thought, but I agree with it. Maturity is more often developed out of our losses than our wins. But *how* you face those losses really matters. People suffer losses, make mistakes, and endure bad experiences all the time without developing maturity.

The Source of Maturity

If you desire to gain the true value of learning that comes through maturity, then keep in mind the following truths:

1. Maturity Is the Result of Finding the Benefit in the Loss

First, you have to *learn* from your mistakes and losses. That's been the common theme throughout this book. Learning is what investor Warren Buffett has done. People today know him as one of the richest men in the world. This elder statesman is well respected for his financial skill and wisdom, but those qualities have come as a result of learning from his losses. He says, "I make plenty of mistakes and I'll make plenty more mistakes, too. That's part of the game. You've just got to make sure that the right things overcome the wrong ones."

Buffett's mistakes include paying too much for businesses (Conoco Phillips and USAir), buying into sinking businesses (Blue Chip Stamp), missing great opportunities (Capital Cities Broadcasting), hiring poor managers, and running operations himself when he shouldn't have. Yet one of the reasons he is so successful in the face of his losses is that he learns from his mistakes but he doesn't dwell on them. I believe the key to being free from the stranglehold of past failures and mistakes is to learn the lesson and forget the details. That brings not only mental advancement but emotional freedom.

Learning from our mistakes is wonderful, but it means little if you don't know how to turn the lesson into a *benefit*. That comes when we take what we've learned and apply it to our future actions. That's what I have tried to do, though it took me a while to learn how to do it. Here are some examples of difficulties I faced, how they affected me emotionally, and how I tried to change my thinking and find the benefit of the experience:

- **When I was over my head writing a Bible commentary:** I felt discouraged, I wanted to quit, and I defined myself as soft. However, I kept working, I got help, and I acquired new ways to learn. Two years later I finished the project. The benefit of the experience: I redefined myself as tenacious. And I never again allowed the challenges of a writing project to prevent me from following through and finishing it.

- **When I had a heart attack:** I realized I had taken my health for granted. I defined myself as undisciplined, and I worried about what the future might hold. But I allowed the experience to change the way I ate and exercised. I began to swim daily. I redefined myself as disciplined in this area for the first time in my life. The benefit: I am living a healthy life every day so that I have additional years with Margaret, our children, and our grandchildren.

- **When my mother died:** I lost the person who gave me unconditional love every day for the first sixty-two years of my life. I was overcome. I felt lost. How many people have someone like that in their lives? And to lose that! But then I realized what a gift she was, and I felt grateful. The benefit: I determined to be that unconditionally loving person in more people's lives.

- **When I lost a million dollars in a bad business decision:** I felt sick because we had to sell some investments to cover the losses, and we couldn't really afford it. I chastised myself because I thought I had been too careless. The benefit: I made some necessary changes in my decision-making process, and I felt much wiser because of the experience.

These key experiences changed me. They taught me lessons, and I benefitted when I applied those lessons. When I was young, I mistakenly thought that as I got older and gained experience, I would make fewer mistakes and suffer few losses. That hasn't been true. What I've discovered is that I still make mistakes and face losses, but I learn more quickly from them and am able to move on much more quickly on an emotional level.

If you want to gain the benefits learned from your losses and mistakes, don't allow them to take you captive emotionally. Banker and speaker Herbert V. Prochnow asserted, "The fellow who never makes a mistake takes his orders from one who does." Why? Because the person who advances in his or her career takes risks, fails, learns, and applies the lesson to gain the benefit. Observe any successful person, and you'll see someone who doesn't see a mistake as the enemy. If they have any regrets, they are likely to be like that of actress Tallulah Bankhead, who said, "If I had my life to live over again, I'd make the same mistakes, only sooner."

2. Maturity Is the Result of Learning to Feed the Right Emotions

Many years ago I came across a verse that I feel accurately describes the human condition. It says,

> *Two natures beat within my breast.*
> *The one is foul, the other blessed.*
> *The one I love, the other I hate,*
> *The one I feed will dominate.*[1]

I believe both positive and negative emotions are contained within each of us. There are people who teach that we should try to eliminate all negative feelings from our lives, but I have never been able to do that. I have tried, but I found that I simply can't. However, what I *can* do is feed the positive thoughts until they become dominant over the negative ones.

It's said that General George Patton, a fearless warrior of the U.S. Army during World War II, thought of himself as anything but brave. When an official praised his acts of heroism, Patton's response was, "Sir, I am not a brave man. The truth of the matter is I am usually a coward at heart. I have never been in the sound of gunshot or sight of battle in my whole life that I was not afraid. I constantly have sweat on my palms and a lump in my throat." How was someone so afraid able to be so brave? He fed the right emotions. Or as Patton put it himself: "I learned very early in life not to take counsel of my fears."

I try to feed the right emotions within myself by *acting* on the emotion that I want to win. "Do something every day that you don't want to do," advised author Mark Twain. "This is the golden rule for acquiring the habit of doing your duty without pain." Acting on the right emotion will lift you to success. Acting on the wrong emotion will lower you to failure.

> "Maturity is doing what you are supposed to be doing, when you're supposed to be doing it, no matter how you feel."
> —*Dom Capers*

I once had lunch with Dom Capers, the successful NFL coach. One of the things he said during our conversation was, "Maturity is doing what you are supposed to be doing, when you're supposed to be doing it, no matter how you feel." That's true. The key to success is action. Too often we want to feel our way into acting, when instead we need to act our way into feeling. If we do the right thing, we will eventually feel the right feelings.

3. Maturity Is the Result of Learning to Develop Good Habits

Og Mandino, author of *The Greatest Salesman in the World*, said, "In truth, the only difference between those who have failed and those who have succeeded lies in the difference of their habits." By encouraging the right emotions within us through positive action over a sustained period of time, we can actually form the habit of taking the right action. And that often leads to further positive results. As poet John Dryden put it: "We first make our habits, and then our habits make us."

In *Life's Greatest Lessons*, Hal Urban writes about the power of good habits. He says,

> The original meaning of *habit* was "garment," or "piece of clothing." And as with garments, we wear our habits daily. Our personalities are actually a composite of our attitudes, habits, and appearance. In other words, our personalities are the characteristics by which we're identified, the parts of us which we reflect to others. As with our clothes, all of our habits are acquired. We're not born with any of them. We learn them, just as we learn our attitudes. They develop over time and are reinforced through repetition.[2]

Good habits require discipline and time to develop. Urban goes on to describe how Benjamin Franklin developed the habits he thought would improve him. Franklin listed thirteen qualities he desired to possess, ranked them in order of importance, and then gave each its own page in a small notebook. He would concentrate on one quality each week, making notes in his little book. In time, he developed the qualities he admired, and it changed him from who he was to who he desired to be.

People in high-pressure careers seem to learn this lesson early, or they don't reach the highest levels of success. For example, in professional ice skating, they call it "staying in your program." When a skater is doing a routine, if he makes a mistake or takes a fall, he is supposed to immediately get up and jump right back into his program—whether he's competing in the Olympics in front of hawk-eyed judges and millions of television watchers or practicing on his own in the early morning hours. It requires focus and the ability to live in the moment. Why is that important? Because to succeed at that high level, you can't allow a challenge to get you off track. You need to cultivate the habit of executing and following through.

If we want to gain the value of learning, we need to be in the habit of executing at a high level, rain or shine, success or failure, setback or breakthrough. We need to heed the advice of Nobel Peace Prize winner Fridtjof Nansen, who said, "Have you not succeeded? Continue! Have you succeeded? Continue!"

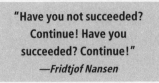
"Have you not succeeded? Continue! Have you succeeded? Continue!"
—Fridtjof Nansen

4. Maturity Is the Result of Learning to Sacrifice Today to Succeed Tomorrow

I've touched on this point before, but it bears repeating. There is a definite connection between success and a person's willingness to make sacrifices. Author Arthur C. Brooks recently wrote an opinion column for the *Wall Street Journal* that addressed this subject. In it, Brooks states, "People who cannot defer current gratification tend to fail, and sacrifice itself is part of entrepreneurial success." He cites a study from 1972 in which Stanford psychologist Walter Mischel conducted an experiment involving small children and marshmallows. Researchers offered the children a marshmallow but stated they could receive a second one if they waited fifteen minutes without eating the first. Two-thirds of the children failed to wait.

One of the most intriguing things about the study was what researchers discovered later. When they followed up on the children to see how their lives were turning out, they found that the children who had delayed gratification scored on average 210 points higher on the SAT, were less likely to drop out of college, made a higher income, and suffered from fewer drug and alcohol problems.

Brooks goes on to explain some of the implications of the research. He writes,

But the evidence goes beyond a finding that people who can defer gratification tend to turn out well in general.

When we hear about successful entrepreneurs, it is always as if they had the Midas touch. A pimply college kid cooks up an Internet company during a boring lecture at Harvard, and before lunch he's a billionaire. In real life, that's not how it works. Northwestern University Professor Steven Rogers has shown that the average entrepreneur fails about four times before succeeding.

When asked about their ultimate success, entrepreneurs often talk instead about the importance of their hardships.... When I asked the legendary investment company founder Charles Schwab about the success of the $15 billion corporation that bears his name, he told me the story about taking out a second mortgage on his home just to make payroll in the early years.

Why this emphasis on the struggle? Entrepreneurs know that when they sacrifice, they are learning and improving, exactly what they need to do to earn success through their merits. Every sacrifice and deferred gratification makes them wiser and better, showing them that they're not getting anything free. When success ultimately comes, they wouldn't trade away the earlier days for anything, even if they felt wretched at the time.[3]

Willingness to sacrifice does not come easily. People naturally tend to adopt behaviors that make them feel good. Everyone likes comfort, pleasure, and entertainment, and they tend to want to reexperience them. If we do this repeatedly, we can become addicted or bored and seek greater pleasures. For some people, this becomes a lifelong pursuit. But there's a problem with that. A person who cannot sacrifice will never belong to himself; he belongs to whatever he was unwilling to give up. If you want to develop maturity and gain the value of learning, you need to learn to give up some things today for greater gains tomorrow.

> If you want to develop maturity and gain the value of learning, you need to learn to give up some things today for greater gains tomorrow.

5. Maturity Is the Result of Learning to Earn Respect for Yourself and Others

Our children are grown and married now with their own families, but when they were teenagers Margaret and I sometimes met with a counselor friend of ours. We both felt the weight of responsibility that accompanies parenting, and we benefited from her advice. During one of those sessions, she scolded me, saying, "You're too affirming with your children, and you want to help them too quickly when they have problems."

I was surprised by her statement and became defensive. "How could anyone be *too* affirming?" I asked. "And why shouldn't a parent jump in and help his children with their problems?"

She knew I believed positive self-worth to be very important in a person's life. She also knew that I wanted to be supportive to my children. But her concern was that I was fostering false self-esteem in them.

"Look," she said, "you can tell your children that they are wonderful all day long, whether they are or not, and it might make them feel good. But then they will go out into the real world expecting the same type of treatment from others, and they will get crushed." Her words rang true to me. She continued, "The best way to enhance the self-esteem in the lives of your children is to give them tools that they can use to better their lives."

Her admonition was confirmed by Margaret. It was true that I did want to shield my family from problems. From that day on, I worked hard to change. I realized that I couldn't give my children self-esteem. I could love them unconditionally, but they had to find their self-esteem themselves through their actions and choices. (And by the way, if you grew up with affirming parents, be grateful, but be determined to perform with excellence, take responsibility for yourself when you don't succeed, and learn from your failures without being defensive.)

The word *esteem* means "to appreciate the worth of, to hold in high regard, to have genuine respect." So *self-esteem* really means "self-respect." That comes from our character. We feel good about ourselves when we make right choices regardless of the circumstances. In fact, if our behavior is positive in the face of negative circumstances, it builds character and self-respect. This comes from inside each of us. And the better prepared we are to face our problems, the greater the maturity and the chance that we can learn and grow.

Author and speaker Brian Tracy says, "Self-esteem is the reputation you have with yourself." If you want it to be solid and lasting, it must be earned and confirmed, day by day. It happens from the inside out. And when it's solid, you know that external forces that come against you aren't going to shake it. You stay true to who you are to the core, you learn from your mistakes, and you keep moving forward.

Fifty Years of Learning the Hard Way

For more than fifty years, Gail Borden Jr. was not a successful man, though it certainly wasn't for lack of trying. Born in 1801, Borden spent his childhood growing up in New York, Indiana, and Mississippi. He received very little formal education, attending school for only two years in his teens. He learned the trade of surveying, and for a while in his midtwenties, he worked as the county surveyor in Amite, Mississippi. But he grew restless there, and when he was twenty-eight he moved to Texas, following his father and brother. For a while, he farmed and raised livestock, but that wasn't what he ultimately wanted to do. So when he got the opportunity to replace his brother as official surveyor in Stephen F. Austin's colony, headquartered at San Felipe, he took the position. But that didn't last long either.

In his midthirties, Borden went into partnership with his brother and a third man to start a newspaper—despite none of them having any printing experience. They published their first issue just days after the start of the Texas Revolution. They published the first list of Texans who died at the Alamo, and they popularized the rallying cry, "Remember the Alamo."

During the Texas Revolution, they fled the Mexican army with their printing press, but had it captured anyway. The soldiers threw the press into Buffalo Bayou. Shortly after the end of the revolution, Borden mortgaged his land to purchase a new printing press, but because of financial difficulties, he ended up selling his interest in the paper.

That was when Borden used his political connections to secure a position in government. Sam Houston appointed Borden as collector of customs in Galveston. Though Borden experienced some success in the position, he was replaced by Sam Houston's successor. So he tried his hand at real estate.

To Some, Maturity Comes Late

To his credit, Borden never gave up. He displayed great tenacity. But one of the strongest criticisms leveled against him was that he lost interest in his endeavors too quickly and would jump to a new interest. As he approached age fifty, a level of maturity finally seemed to be setting in. In the 1840s, he started inventing. When he learned about the California Gold Rush, he concentrated his full attention on condensing foods so that they could be preserved for long periods of time. Borden said, "I mean to put a potato into a pillbox, a pumpkin into a tablespoon, and a watermelon into a saucer."

Borden's first effort was what he called a meat biscuit. He extracted all the nutrients from beef by boiling it. He then strained the liquid and condensed it into a syrup, which he mixed with flour and baked into a dry biscuit. He eventually patented the process, and it was successful enough for him to receive a contract to produce the biscuits for the

United States Army. He also received a Council medal at the Great Exhibition in London in 1851. But his greatest contribution to society ended up being a different product.

Onboard ship returning from England, Borden saw children die as a result of drinking contaminated milk. He vowed to find a way to condense milk and preserve it so that it would be safe for human consumption.

At first he approached the task in a way similar to how he had created the meat biscuit. He put milk in a kettle and boiled off the water, but the process failed. The milk tasted burned. He tried other approaches, but it wasn't until he saw maple sugar condensed in a vacuum-sealed pan that he discovered the process that worked. He had finally found success, but by that time he was nearly ruined financially. So he took on partners. With their help, he was able to open a factory in Connecticut in 1856. However, when the operation didn't see an immediate profit, the investors withdrew and the facility closed down. With the help of another investor, Borden opened another facility. It too shut down because of a nationwide financial crisis.

Many people would have given up at this point. In fact, had these events happened earlier in Borden's life, he probably would have given up. But by this time he had finally developed enough maturity to learn from his losses and seize opportunity when it presented itself. When Borden met financier Jeremiah Milbank on a train, Borden convinced him to become his partner. They founded the New York Condensed Milk Company in 1857, which was finally successful. Later, it was renamed the Borden Company. Milbank's investment of $100,000 was said to be worth $8 million when he died in 1884.

Condensed milk became the means of Borden's fortune. He developed other processes to preserve food, such as one to condense fruit juices. But it is for condensed milk that he will always be remembered. And his life is a testament to the value of learning when a person finally matures and absorbs the lessons of loss, mistakes, and failure. It was a lesson Borden learned well. On his tombstone he asked that the following words be inscribed: "I tried and failed. I tried again and succeeded." What more could a person be expected to do?

13

Winning Isn't Everything,
But Learning Is

I remember reading a *For Better or Worse* comic strip in which a boy is playing chess with his grandfather. "Oh, no! Not again!" cries the boy. "Grandpa, you always win!"

"What do you want me to do," answers his grandfather, "lose on purpose? You won't learn anything if I do that."

"I don't wanna learn anything," complains the boy. "I just wanna win!"

As well as anything I've ever seen, that captures how most of us feel. We just want to win! But the truth is that winning isn't everything—learning is.

Final Thoughts on Learning

Author Doug Adams said, "You live and learn. At any rate you live." It is possible to win and not learn. However, for the person who puts winning ahead of learning, life will be difficult.

My purpose in writing this book has been to help you to learn

213

how to learn—from your losses, failures, mistakes, challenges, and bad experiences. I want you to become a continual winner by being a habitual learner. To help you with that, I want to share some final thoughts on learning to help guide you as you go forward.

1. Learning Too Often Decreases as Winning Increases

Several years ago over dinner in Odessa, Texas, I had a conversation with Jim Collins, author of *Good to Great*. Jim is a good thinker, and I enjoy discussing leadership with him. At that time, the economy was humming and unemployment was running under 4 percent. We talked about the danger of complacency anytime people are winning. They are tempted to relax and sit back when things are going well. And Jim posed a question: "How do we continue to grow and improve and become more, when what we already have is pretty good?"

Complacency: that is the danger any successful person faces.

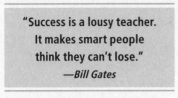

"Success is a lousy teacher. It makes smart people think they can't lose."
—*Bill Gates*

Microsoft founder Bill Gates observed, "Success is a lousy teacher. It makes smart people think they can't lose." It also makes them think they don't need to learn.

The biggest detriment to tomorrow's success is today's success. That problem can manifest itself in many ways. Here are the ones I've observed most often:

- *Been There, Done That:* Some people hit a milestone, and they make it a tombstone. They get bored, lose their curiosity, and disengage. Don't let that happen to you.
- *The Banquet Tour:* When you succeed, people want to hear your story. However, there's a real danger that you can replace

doing with speaking. Consultant Gail Cooper advises, "When you win an award, set it up in the lobby and go back to work."

- *Success Guarantees Success:* Just because you can do one thing well doesn't mean you can do all things well. When you win, maintain your perspective.
- *The Momentum Myth:* People's natural inclination after a win is to take a break. Bad idea. When you're winning, capitalize on the momentum. You'll be able to do things that might otherwise be impossible.
- *One-Hit Wonders:* Have you ever known someone who was successful *once*—and is still living off of it? It's a good idea to *build* off of yesterday; it's a bad idea to *live* off of it.
- *The Entitlement Mind-set:* People who have something that they didn't win for themselves start thinking they are entitled to more. That's why many inherited businesses go *out* of business. To keep winning, you need to stay hungry and keep learning.
- *Playing Not to Lose:* After some people win, they become cautious and defensive. They worry about staying on top. Not wanting to do something stupid, they do something stupid; they focus on not losing instead of winning.
- *The Arrival Plateau:* Some people become so focused on a specific goal that when they hit it they give up, because they believe they've made it. That mind-set has the power to unmake them.

Any one of these wrong attitudes toward winning can turn a person from winner to loser very quickly. You've probably heard the phrase, "The number one rule of winning is don't beat yourself!" These are some of the most common ways people get off track once they've achieved some level of success. Novelist John Steinbeck gives some insight into why this happens. In a letter to Adlai Stevenson published in the *Washington Post* on January 28, 1960, Steinbeck wrote, "A strange species we are. We can stand anything God and nature throw at us save only plenty. If I wanted to destroy a nation, I would give it too much, and I would have it on its knees: miserable, greedy, and sick."

> The number one rule of winning is don't beat yourself!

If you want to keep learning and growing, you need to stay hungry. Depending on your personality, winning may remove some of your hunger to win again. So instead, keep your hunger to learn. Then no matter whether you win or lose, you'll keep getting better.

2. Learning Is Possible Only When Our Thinking Changes

Have you ever wondered why so many people who win the lottery lose all of their money? It happens continually. One day they're holding a check worth millions, and a few years later they've lost it all. Why is that? The reason they lose their money is that they don't change their thinking. They may receive new money, but they hold on to their same old thinking. It's not what we have that determines our success. It's how we think. If they'd give up their thinking, then they might hold on to their money.

I've noticed three particular positive thinking patterns of people who are always learning. Adopt them and you will be able to keep changing your thinking in a way to keep you learning:

Don't Let What You Know Make You Think that You Know It All

Writer and philosopher J. Krishnamurti asserted, "To know is to be ignorant. Not to know is the beginning of wisdom." As you win,

and learn and grow, you face a genuine danger of thinking you know it
all. Don't let that happen! You simply
can't learn what you think you already
know.

> "To know is to be ignorant.
> Not to know is the
> beginning of wisdom."
> —*J. Krishnamurti*

I've worked hard to protect myself from falling into this trap. I
began my passionate study of leadership in 1974. In the nearly four
decades since then, I've read thousands of leadership articles and
books, met thousands of leaders, attended hundreds of leadership
events, dealt with continual leadership issues, written hundreds of
leadership lessons, spoken to millions of people on this subject, and
written over seventy books. Have I arrived? No! I'm still a student of
leadership, and I'm still challenged to become a better leader.

One of the things that keeps me excited about learning new leadership thoughts is my passion for the subject. I'm still asking other
leaders questions about leadership. I'm still exploring. I'm not close to
knowing everything about it, and I don't think I ever will be. I don't
want to be close. I want to die asking questions and still wanting to
learn more. You should be just as passionate about whatever it is you
were put on this earth to do. If you can maintain a beginner's mind-
set to the end, your thinking will keep changing and you will keep
growing.

Maintain a Positive Mental Attitude

Writer and thinker G. K. Chesterton said, "How we think when we
lose determines how long it will be until we win." I believe a key part
of the right kind of thinking comes from remaining positive. How do
you do that? By continually feeding positive thoughts to your mind
by reading positive books, collecting positive quotes, and listening to

positive messages. When you do that, you supply your thinking with plenty of positive material, and you keep your mind focused on things that will encourage you.

When negative ideas and discouraging thoughts want to creep in and make you negative, you will have already created a barrier to them. Think positively long enough, and not only will your positive thoughts be stronger than your negative ones, they will be more comfortable, too.

Maintaining a consistently positive mental attitude will be your greatest ally in growing and learning. If you can remain positive, then even when things go wrong, you won't break a sweat. Your attitude will be, *The worst thing that could happen to me today could lead to the best thing that happens today.*

> **Maintaining a consistently positive mental attitude will be your greatest ally in growing and learning.**

Embrace Creativity in Every Situation

There's a classic brainteaser showing the power of creative thinking that I have sometimes shared with people when I teach. Here it is: using four straight lines, connect all nine dots below without crossing the same dot twice or lifting your pencil from the paper.

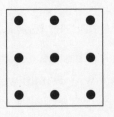

Did you solve it? Most people have a hard time with it the first time they try it. The secret is that you have to *got outside of the box!* (If you're still not sure how to solve it, you can find the solution at the end of the chapter.)

Going outside of the box is the key to much of the creative thinking that can help you to keep growing and learning. The problem is that most of us believe we are *supposed* to stay inside the box, remain inside the lines, and so forth. Who says so? There should be no restrictions to the way we think or how we approach problem solving.

Creativity is the ability to free yourself from imaginary boundaries, to see new relationships, and to explore options so that you can accomplish more things of value. What holds people back from their potential is all the "imaginary boundaries" they have allowed to imprison their thinking and doing. Wonderful, workable options are the rewards for becoming more creative. Greater learning comes from better thinking. That requires us to change.

3. Real Learning Is Defined as a Change in Behavior

Humorist Will Rogers said, "There are three kinds of men. Ones that learn by reading, a few who learn by observation, and the rest of us have to pee on an electric fence and find out for ourselves." Ouch. That's got to hurt. But let's face it: some people only learn things the hard way.

I've heard author and consultant Ken Blanchard say, "You haven't learned anything until you take action and use it." In my opinion, that's the right perspective when it comes to learning. It's measured by tangible action. That's why coach John Wooden used to continually say to his players, "Don't tell me what you're going to do, show me what you will do."

The greatest gap in life is the one between knowing and doing. I can't count the number of people I've met who *know* what they are supposed to do, yet don't take action on it. Sometimes it's due to fear.

Other times to laziness. Other times to emotional dysfunction. The problem is that knowing what to do and *not* doing it is no better than not knowing what to do. It ends in the same result. Stagnation. You haven't really learned something until you've lived it. Or as poet Ralph Waldo Emerson said, "Life is a succession of lessons which must be lived to be understood."

My friend Dave Ramsey, a financial expert who writes books, teaches seminars, and hosts a syndicated radio show, places a very high premium on action when he teaches and counsels people about money and finances. During a recent interview he pointed out, "What I found is that personal finance is 80 percent behavior. Everybody tries to fix financial problems with math. But it's not a math problem, and it's not a knowledge problem. It's a behavior problem. The problem with my money is the idiot I shave with every morning. If I can get that guy in the mirror to behave, he can be skinny and rich. It's not magic."[1] That's true. Turning learning into changed behavior isn't magic. But it is magical. It can change your life.

4. Continual Success Is a Result of Continually Failing and Learning

Chicago teacher Marva Collins says, "If you can't make a mistake, you can't make anything." How true. If you want to be successful, you

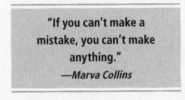
"If you can't make a mistake, you can't make anything."
—*Marva Collins*

must be willing to fail, and you must be intent on learning from those failures. If we are willing to repeat this fail-and-learn process, we become stronger and better than we were before.

In his book *Life's Greatest Lessons*, Hal Urban describes this process. He calls it "Strong at the Broken Places." Urban writes,

Near the end of *A Farewell to Arms*, Ernest Hemingway's famous novel about World War I, he wrote, "The world breaks everyone and afterward many are strong at the broken places." The world does, indeed, break everyone, and usually not just once. But as a broken bone becomes even stronger when it heals, so do we. It all depends on our attitude and our choices. We can become stronger at our broken places if we choose to learn from our mistakes, correct our course, and try again. Our failures in life, as painful as they are, can be our most valuable learning experiences and our greatest source of renewed strength. As General George S. Patton said, "Success is how high you bounce after you hit bottom."[2]

My hope for you is that you will bounce high—and keep bouncing. With each successive bounce back, you'll be able to go higher and farther. That's what success in life is: the learned ability to keep bouncing back. As author and entrepreneur Joseph Sugarman says, "If you're willing to accept failure and learn from it, if you're willing to consider failure as a blessing in disguise and bounce back, you've got the potential of harnessing one of the most powerful success forces."

> "If you're willing to consider failure as a blessing in disguise and bounce back, you've got the potential of harnessing one of the most powerful success forces."
> —Joseph Sugarman

Focus and Risk as You Win, Lose, and Learn

As you move forward in life and work to achieve success, remember that progress requires risk, leads to failure, and provides many learning opportunities. Anytime you try something new, you must risk.

That's just a part of learning. But there's an art to managing that risk, and it comes from successfully coordinating the two zones for success that you have in your life: your strength zone, where you do your best work; and your comfort zone, where you feel safe.

To maximize your success, you must make the most of your successes and failures. To do that, you need to get in your strength zone but get out of your comfort zone. Take a look at how this works:

STRENGTH ZONE	COMFORT ZONE	RESULT
Outside Your Strength Zone	Outside Your Comfort Zone	Poor Performance— Winning is Impossible
Outside Your Strength Zone	Inside Your Comfort Zone	Mediocre Performance— Winning is Impossible
Inside Your Strength Zone	Inside Your Comfort Zone	Good Performance— Winning is Possible
Inside Your Strength Zone	Outside Your Comfort Zone	Great Performance— Winning is Continual

Traditional wisdom and, frankly, the focus of most education, is to shore up your weaknesses. But that's not where you will do your best work. People don't succeed if they focus their time and effort outside of their strength zone. You have to major in your strengths. That's where your productivity resides. The recent work of the Gallup organization bears this out and is discussed extensively in the Strengths Finder books and testing instruments they've published.

While it's true that your greatest successes will be in your strength zone, it's also true that your best failures will occur there. Why do I say that? Because you'll recover the fastest and learn the most where your talent and skills are strongest. For example, one of my greatest strengths is communication. Let's say I try something new onstage when I'm speaking to an audience, and it fails miserably. I will probably be able to figure out what went wrong very quickly. I might even be able to diagnose the problem and make the necessary adjustments while I'm still on stage speaking. And because I'm working in my strength, I'll understand the problem and won't repeat what I did wrong.

In contrast, let's say I have a problem with my car. I'm driving down the road and it quits on me. The only thing I know how to do in that situation is check the fuel gauge. If that's not the problem, I have absolutely no chance of figuring out how to fix it. The only thing I can do in that situation is call my mechanic. And even if he explains *exactly* what was wrong, there won't be anything I can do about it if it happens again in the future. Why? Because it's totally out of my strength zone.

I'm sure the process is similar for you. If you're outside of your strength zone, a problem is a mystery. If you're in your strength zone, a problem is a challenge, a learning experience, and a road to improvement. That's why you need to get out of your comfort zone by taking risks while working in your strength zone. When you take risks, you learn things faster than the people who don't take risks. You experiment. You learn more about what works and what doesn't. You overcome obstacles more quickly than the people who play it safe and are able to build on those experiences.

Political theorist Benjamin Barber said, "I divide the world into learners and nonlearners. There are people who learn, who are open to what happens around them, who listen, who hear the lessons. When they do something stupid, they don't do it again. And when they do something that works a little bit, they do it even better and harder the next time. The question to ask is not whether you are a success or a failure, but whether you are a learner or a nonlearner."

Keep Climbing

The greatest education you ever receive will come from taking risks in your area of strength. Risk taking without ability leads to increased frustration and continual failure. Risk taking with ability leads to increased learning and success.

I don't know what your personal Mount Everest is—what you were put on this earth to do. Everybody has one. But I do know this: win or lose, you need to try to reach the summit. If you don't, you will always regret it. As you get older, you will find that you become more disappointed by the things you didn't attempt than by the ones you tried and failed to achieve. And here's the best news. Every step of the way there's something to learn. You are enrolled in a full-time informal school called life. In it, there are no mistakes, only lessons. Growth is a process of trial and error, experimentation and improvement. The failed experiments are as much of that process as the ones that work.

The lessons you have the opportunity to learn will be presented to you in various forms. Fail to learn the lesson and you get stuck, unable to move forward. Learn the lesson and you get to move forward and go to the next one. And if you do it right, the process never ends. There is no part of life that doesn't contain lessons. If you're alive, that means you still have opportunities ahead of you to learn. You just have to be willing to tackle them. You have all the tools and resources you need. The choice is yours. Others will give you advice. Some may even help you, But you have to take the test. Sometimes you will win. Sometimes you will lose. But every time you will have the opportunity to ask yourself, "What did I learn?" If you always have an answer to that question, then you will go far. And you will enjoy the journey.

Solution to the puzzle on page 218:

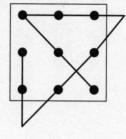

Notes

1. When You're Losing, Everything Hurts

1. Charles Bracelen Flood, *Lee: The Last Years* (New York: Mariner Books, 1998), 136.

2. Humility: The Spirit of Learning

1. "John Wooden: Life and Times," UCLA, http://www.spotlight.ucla.edu/john-wooden/life-and-times/, accessed 23 September 2010.
2. John Wooden and Don Yeager, *A Game Plan for Life: The Power of Mentoring* (New York: Bloomsbury, 2009), 34.
3. Jim Tressel with Chris Fabry, *The Winners Manual: For the Game of Life* (Carol Stream, IL: Tyndale, 2008), 157.
4. Norman McGowan, *My Years With Churchill* (London: Souvenir Press, 1958).
5. Eccles. 7:14 (NASB).
6. Charlotte Foltz Jones, *Mistakes That Worked* (New York: Doubleday, 1991), introduction.
7. Ibid., 8–9.
8. Ibid., 51–53.
9. "Accidental Discoveries," Xperimania, http://www.xperimania.net/ww/en/pub/xperimania/news/world_of_materials/accidental_discoveries.htm, accessed July 20, 2012.
10. Letter dated August 20, 1816, Image 58 of 360, Bound Volume, 30 January 1816–28 December 1818, "The Samuel F. B. Morse Papers at the Library of Congress," Library of Congress, http://memory.loc.gov/cgi-bin/ampage?collId=mmorse&fileName=005/005001/005001page.db&recNum=57, accessed July 12, 2012.
11. Letter dated September 2, 1816, Images 70–72 of 360, Bound Volume, 30 January 1816–28 December 1818, "The Samuel F. B. Morse Papers at the Library of Congress," Library of Congress, http://memory.loc.gov/

cgi-bin/ampage?collId=mmorse&fileName=005/005001/005001page
.db&recNum=69, accessed July 13, 2012.

12. Tim Hansel, *Eating Problems for Breakfast* (Waco, TX: Word Publishing,
1988) 33–34.

3. Reality: The Foundation of Learning

1. Charlene Schiff, "Charlene Schiff: A Daughter's Separation from Her
Mother," First Person Podcast Series (transcript), United States Holocaust
Memorial Museum, http://www.ushmm.org/museum/publicprograms/
programs/firstperson/podcast/detail.php?EventId=E6E7C692-DFC9
-49E3-8577-7E495EEFD0B7&lang=en, accessed August 10, 2012.

2. Charlene Schiff as told to Sam Boykin, in "Home of the Brave," *Reader's
Digest*, April 2009, 149.

3. "Survivor Volunteers: Charlene Schiff (Shulamit Perlmutter)," United States
Holocaust Memorial Museum, http://www.ushmm.org/remembrance/
survivoraffairs/meet/detail.php?content=schiff, accessed August 10, 2012.

4. "Charlene Schiff: A Daughter's Separation."

5. "Survivor Volunteers: Charlene Schiff (Shulamit Perlmutter)."

6. "Ibid.

7. Boykin, "Home of the Brave."

8. Jack Moline, "A Life Bearing Witness to the Holocaust," *Alexandria
Gazette Packet*, November 5, 2008, http://www.tisaraphoto.com/legends/
Schiff.htm, accessed July 30, 2012.

9. Boykin, "Home of the Brave."

10. Hal Urban, *Life's Greatest Lessons: 20 Things That Matter* (New York:
Fireside, 2003), 12.

11. Source unknown.

12. Michael Tarm, "Astronauts, Flight Directors Hold Reunion to Mark 40th
Anniversary of Apollo 13 Drama, Triumph," *Star Tribune*, April 12, 2010,
http://www.startribune.com/templates/Print_This_Story?sid=90707004,
accessed April 5, 2013.

4. Responsibility: The First Step of Learning

1. Spongebob623, "Homeless Man w/Golden Radio Voice," YouTube, http://
www.youtube.com/watch?v=HoXS2MSPFwI.

2. Ted Williams with Bret Witter, *A Golden Voice: How Faith, Hard Work,
and Humility Brought Me from the Streets to Salvation* (New York: Gotham
Books, 2012), 23.

3. Ibid., 37.

4. Ibid., 53.

5. Ibid., 55.

6. Ibid., 161.

7. Ibid., 251.

8. Charles J. Sykes, *A Nation of Victims: The Decay of the American Character* (New York: St. Martin's Griffin, 1993), 3.

9. *A Golden Voice*, 237.

10. Matthew 5:45.

11. Author unknown.

12. " 'Thank You for Smoking' author Christopher Buckley Takes on Social Security Reform in 'Boomsday,' " Greater Talent Network," http://www.greater talent.com/speaker-news/thank-you-for-smoking-author-christopher -buckley-takes-on-social-security-reform-in-boomsday/, accessed August 23, 2012.

13. Eric Plasker, "I Choose My Life," in *The 100 Year Lifestyle* (Avon, MA: Adams Media, 2007), Kindle edition, location 4686–4711 of 4808.

14. Patricia Sellers, "So You Fail. Now Bounce Back!" CNNMoney, May 1, 1995, http://money.cnn.com/magazines/fortune/fortune_archive/1995/05/01/ 202473/index.htm, accessed August 27, 2012.

15. Alan Loy McGinnis, *Confidence: How to Succeed at Being Yourself* (Minneapolis, MN: Augsburg Fortress, 1987), 27.

16. Frances Cole Jones, *The Wow Factor: The 33 Things You Must (and Must Not) Do to Guarantee Your Edge in Today's Business World* (New York: Ballantine Books, 2009), 30–31.

5. Improvement: The Focus of Learning

1. "Walter Cronkite," obituary, *New York Times*, July 17, 2009, http://www .legacy.com/obituaries/nytimes/obituary.aspx?page=lifestory&pid=129897 828#fbLoggedOut, accessed August 28, 2012.

2. Richard Huff, "Walter Cronkite, 'Most Trusted Man in America' and CBS Anchor, Dead at 92," New York *Daily News*, July 17, 2009, http://articles .nydailynews.com/2009-07-17/news/17929428_1_anchor-seat-walter -cronkite-cbs-anchor, accessed August 28, 2012.

3. Dana Cook, "Walter Cronkite, 1916–2009," *Salon*, July 18, 2009, http:// www.salon.com/2009/07/18/walter_cronkite/, accessed August 28, 2012.

4. Walter Cronkite, *A Reporter's Life* (New York: Ballantine Books, 1996), 68.

5. Henry O. Dormann, comp., *Letters from Leaders: Personal Advice for Tomorrow's Leaders from the World's Most Influential People* (Guilford, CT: Lyons Press, 2009) 22–23.

6. Kevin Kelly, "The Speed of Information," *The Technium* (blog), February 20, 2006, http://www.kk.org/thetechnium/archives/2006/02/the_speed_of_in.php, accessed August 29, 2012.

7. "Author Biography: Jack V. Matson," Paradigm Press, http://www.innseren dipity.com/paradigm/matson.html, accessed August 29, 2012.

6. Hope: The Motivation of Learning

1. Full-page ad placed by Marriott, *USA Today*, January 20, 2009.
2. "When Everything Material is Lost," Pulpit Helps, http://www.pulpithelps .com/www/docs/243-317, accessed September 4, 2012.
3. Jonathan Sacks, *The Dignity of Difference: How to Avoid the Clash of Civilizations* (New York: Continuum, 2002), 206.
4. Bob Wosczyk, *Who Says the Fat Lady Has to Sing? How to Overcome the Eight Fears That Make Us Quit on Our Lifelong Dreams* (Tucson: Wheatmark, 2008), 1–2.
5. Jim Abbott and Tim Brown, *Imperfect: An Improbable Life* (New York: Ballantine Books, 2012), 55.
6. Ibid., 56.
7. Ibid., 58.
8. Ibid., 61.
9. Ibid., 66.
10. Ibid., 182.
11. Ibid., 185.
12. Ibid., 183.
13. "Jim Abbott Career Stats," MLB.com, http://mlb.mlb.com/team/player .jsp?player_id=110009, accessed September 10, 2012.
14. Abbott and Brown, *Imperfect*, 276.

7. Teachability: The Pathway of Learning

1. Mark Murphy, *Hiring for Attitude: A Revolutionary Approach to Recruiting Star Performers with Both Tremendous Skills and Superb Attitude* (New York: McGraw-Hill, 2012), xi–xii.
2. Hal Urban, *Life's Greatest Lessons: 20 Things That Matter* (New York: Fireside, 2003), 42–43.
3. Ibid., 50.
4. Jeorald Pitts and Lil Tone, "Can You Identify What I Am?" *Los Angeles Sentinel*, December 16, 2010, http://www.lasentinel.net/index.php?option=com _content&view=article&id=3252:can-you-identify-what-i-am&catid= 92&Itemid=182, accessed September 13, 2012.
5. Richard Wurmbrand, *In God's Underground*, Kindle edition (Bartlesville, OK: Living Sacrifice Book Company, 1968), location 213 of 3720.
6. Ibid., location 102 of 3720.

8. Adversity: The Catalyst for Learning

1. Gilbert King, "The Unknown Story of the Black Cyclone, the Cycling Champion Who Broke the Color Barrier," *Past Imperfect* (blog), *Smithsonian*, September 12, 2012, http://blogs.smithsonianmag.com/history/2012/09/

the-unknown-story-of-the-black-cyclone-the-cycling-champion
-who-broke-the-color-barrier/?utm_source=smithsoniantopic&utm
_medium=email&utm_campaign=20120916-Weekender, accessed September 17, 2012.

2. Michael Kranish, "Major Taylor—The World's Fastest Bicycle Racer," *Boston Globe Magazine*, September 16, 2001, http://www.michaelkranish.com/ Michael_Kranish/Major_Taylor.html, accessed September 18, 2012.

3. King, "The Unknown Story of the Black Cyclone."

4. Kranish, "Major Taylor."

5. King, "The Unknown Story of the Black Cyclone."

6. Kranish, "Major Taylor."

7. Ibid.

8. Robert Browning Hamilton, "Along the Road," cited in Edith P. Hazen, ed., *The Columbia Granger's Index to Poetry,* 10th edition (New York: Columbia University Press, 1993), 34.

9. Amy Wilkinson, "Entrepreneurial Nation," *USA Today*, July 16, 2009, 9A.

10. James Casey, "Climb the Steep," PoemHunter.com, http://www.poemhunter .com/poem/climb-the-steep/, accessed September 25, 2012.

9. Problems: Opportunities for Learning

1. Source unknown.

2. Robert H. Schuller, *Tough Times Never Last, But Tough People Do* (New York: Bantam Books, 1984), 73.

3. *Understanding the Winds of Adversity*, Supplementary Alumni Book, volume 7 (Oak Brook, IL: Institute in Basic Youth Conflicts, 1981), quoted in Bill Scheidler, "Understanding Suffering and Affliction," ChurchLeadershipRe sources.com, http://www.churchleadershipresources.com/DownloadLand ing.aspx?resourceId=2662&openOrSave=Save, accessed September 28, 2012.

4. Lowell D. Streiker, *An Encyclopedia of Humor* (Peabody, MA: Hendrickson Publishers, 1998), http://www.pdfdocspace.com/docs/31004/an-encyclopedia -of-humor(100).html, accessed September 28, 2012 (page is no longer available).

10. Bad Experiences: The Perspective for Learning

1. Louisa Fletcher Tarkington, "The Land of Beginning Again," cited in Stanley Schell, ed., *Werner's Readings and Recitations*, no. 51 (New York: Edgar S. Werner and Company, 1912), 128, http://books.google.com/books?id =yDAPAQAAMAAJ&pg=PA128&lpg=PA128&dq=land+of+beginning +again+louisa+fletcher+tarkington&source=bl&ots=NAfj_raTbs&sig= c7PH0s_4yLsOO0oUhBEy5FWOL3A&hl=en&sa=X&ei=KiZfUd_IHoP

A9QSm74DoDw&ved=0CF8Q6AEwBw#v=onepage&q=land%20of%20
beginning%20again%20louisa%20fletcher%20tarkington&f=false, accessed
April 5, 2013.

2. Source unknown.

3. Pat Forde, "U.S. Olympic Swim Trials are Exhilarating for Top Two Finishers,
Excruciating If You End Up Third," Yahoo! Sports, June 24, 2012, http://sports
.yahoo.com/news/olympics--u-s--olympic-swim-trials-excruciating-if-you
-finish-third.html, accessed October 1, 2012.

11. Change: The Price of Learning

1. Christopher Bonanos, *Instant: The Story of Polaroid* (New York: Princeton
Architectural Press, 2012), 31.

2. Ibid., 32.

3. Ibid., 32, 34.

4. Ibid., 34.

5. Ibid., 44.

6. Ibid., 7.

7. Ibid., 135.

8. Ibid., 145.

9. Lance Secretan, "Unlearn and Then Dream," *Personal Excellence*, 11,
http://www.calaministries.org/PE_1209_ap.pdf, accessed October 4, 2012
(page is no longer available).

12. Maturity: The Value of Learning

1. Author unknown.

2. Urban, *Life's Greatest Lessons*, 62.

3. Arthur C. Brooks, "Obama's Budget Flunks the Marshmallow Test," *Wall
Street Journal*, February 24, 2012, http://online.wsj.com/article/SB1000142
4052970204880404577229220571408412.html, accessed October 8, 2012.

13. Winning Isn't Everything, But Learning Is

1. Dave Ramsey interview, *Success*, September–October 2006, 40.

2. Urban, *Life's Greatest Lessons*, 156.

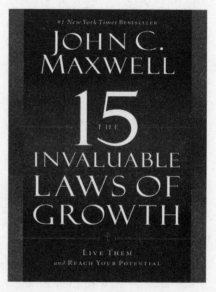

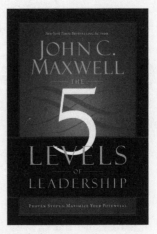

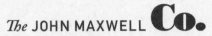